Terror of the Spanish Main

TERROR

of the

SPANISH MAIN

SIR
HENRY
MORGAN
and His
BUCCANEERS

Albert Marrin

DUTTON CHILDREN'S BOOKS
NEW YORK

Illustration Credits
Pages 4, 6, 9, 10, 12–13, 14, 16, 23, 24, 25, 26, 33, 36, 43, 44, 45, 46, 47, 51, 57, 58, 59, 69, 72, 77, 82, 88, 89, 91, 92, 93, 99, 101, 104, 114, 120, 123, 138, 144, 167, 190–91, 193, 215 courtesy of the author; pages 18, 38, 67, 71, 80, 81, 90, 96, 114, 129, 133, 146, 155, 210 courtesy of the Library of Congress; page 65 courtesy of the British Museum; page 119 courtesy of the Hispanic Society of America, New York City; page 227 courtesy of the British Library.

Library of Congress Cataloging-in-Publication Data

Marrin, Albert.
Terror of the Spanish Main: Sir Henry Morgan and his buccaneers/by Albert Marrin.—1st ed.
p.   cm.
Includes bibliographical references (pp. 233–235)
Summary: An account of the life and times of the English buccaneer Henry Morgan from his birth in Wales through his daring exploits in the Spanish Main to his later years in Jamaica.
ISBN 0-525-45942-1
1. Morgan, Henry, Sir, 1635?–1688—Juvenile literature.   2. Spanish Main—Juvenile literature.
3. Panama (Panama)—Destruction, 1671—Juvenile literature.   4. Caribbean Area—
History—to 1810—Juvenile literature.   5. Buccaneers—History—Juvenile literature.
[1. Morgan, Henry, Sir, 1635?–1688.   2. Buccaneers.]   I. Title.
F2161.M83M37   1999   972.9′03′092—dc21   [b]   98-7819   CIP   AC

Published in the United States 1999 by Dutton Children's Books,
a division of Penguin Putnam Books for Young Readers
345 Hudson Street, New York, New York 10014
http://www.penguinputnam.com/yreaders/index.htm

Maps by Richard Amari
Designed by Amy Berniker
Printed in Hong Kong   First Edition
10 9 8 7 6 5 4 3 2 1

To our very dear friends, the Levines:

Jack, Fran, Caren, Noah, Joshua, Theresa,

David, Keith, and Marc

Contents

This is the ballad of Henry Morgan
Who troubled the sleep of the King of Spain
With a frowsy, blowsy, lousy pack
Of the water rats of the Spanish Main,
Rakes and rogues and mad rapscallions
Broken gentlemen, tatterdemallions
Scum and scourge of the hemisphere,
Who looted the loot of the stately galleons,
Led by Morgan, the Buccaneer.

—BERTON BRALEY, 1934

Terror of the Spanish Main

> "Great Morgan's Fame shall last as long as there
> Is beat of Drum, or any Sound of War."
> —anonymous song, c. 1680

Port Royal, Jamaica, the West Indies. A cloudless day with a dazzling sun and a gentle sea breeze rustling the palm trees.

If you happened to find yourself on Thames Street on such a day in the late 1600s, you might have seen Sir Henry Morgan strolling downtown toward the docks. He often came to town from his country estate to meet old cronies, collect money in return for some "favor," or drink rum in one of the sleazy waterfront taverns. Although Morgan had been born a commoner, His Majesty, King Charles II of England, had rewarded him with a knighthood for his exploits against Spain's possessions in the New World.

Sir Henry walked straight ahead, turning neither to the right nor the left. Yet his manner and the way he carried himself showed that very little escaped his sharp eyes. A man of medium height and muscular build, he weighed about 175 pounds, had black hair reaching down to his shoulders, and had a nut brown complexion, the result of many years spent in the tropics. A mustache started thin under his nose and ended in round bulbs at either end; a tuft of hair, just the barest suggestion of a beard, grew under the center part of his lower lip.

Despite the scorching heat and stifling humidity, Sir Henry wore a heavily brocaded coat with raised patterns embroidered in gold thread. In his left hand he carried a three-cornered hat topped by a flowing ostrich plume. The rest of his outfit consisted of a sky blue silk vest trimmed with pearls, white knee-length breeches of linen, white silk stockings tied below the knees with blue ribbons, and chunky high-heeled shoes decorated with silver buckles. A gold hoop earring dangled from each earlobe. A silver-handled sword in a sheath of scarlet velvet flopped against his left hip, and he had a pistol inlaid with ivory and silver thrust into a wide leather belt. Experience had taught the townspeople that he did not carry these weapons for show. This was a man who knew how to give orders, and he expected instant obedience.

"Good morning, Harry," said passersby, tipping their hats. Everyone used the familiar form of his first name. Yet that was the only familiarity they ever took, and the only one he allowed. For Sir Henry Morgan was as close to royalty as citizens of Port Royal were likely to meet this side of heaven or hell. Although not of royal blood, he was a prince of a special type: a prince of buccaneers. That made him the most feared person in the New World. For nearly two decades on behalf of England he had terrorized the Spanish Main, or Spain's colonies on the northeast coast of South America and her mainland possessions bordering the Caribbean Sea and Gulf of Mexico.

· · ·

An artist's impression of Sir Henry Morgan at the height of his fame and power. The ship flies an English naval flag, a red Saint George's cross set against a white background.

Sir Henry Morgan's story began long before that day on Thames Street in Jamaica. In fact, it began over a century before Henry first saw the light of day. It began with Christopher Columbus and a line drawn on a map.

Columbus's return to Spain in March 1493 from his first voyage ignited a dispute that would last nearly two centuries and claim the lives of countless human beings. Insisting that she alone had borne the risks and expenses of exploration, Spain claimed the entire Western Hemisphere—its lands, its peoples, and its wealth—as hers.

Neighboring Portugal, however, objected. During the late Middle Ages, Portuguese seamen ventured farther than any other Europeans had ever dared. Inspired by Prince Henry the Navigator, they had been seeking an all-water route to the spices of the Orient for sixty years before Columbus set sail. While they headed southward along the African coast and then eastward across the Indian Ocean, Columbus struck westward across the Atlantic, only to stumble upon a world new to Europeans. Portugal, however, demanded her "rights," refusing to recognize a Spanish monopoly. Unless Spain allowed her to explore the (as yet) unknown lands, she threatened to declare war.

Both sides appealed to the pope in Rome. As head of the Roman Catholic Church, to which all Christians in Western Europe owed allegiance, the Holy Father was supposed to represent God on Earth. When he spoke, the faithful believed the Lord spoke through his lips. And when he made a decision, it had the force of divine law, as binding in Heaven as on Earth. For centuries, popes had peacefully settled disputes between European rulers.

In May 1493, Pope Alexander VI unrolled a parchment map on a large marble-topped table. Dipping his pen into a jeweled

During the early 1400s, Prince Henry of Portugal, also called Henry the Navigator, spent almost every waking moment directing voyages of discovery along the west coast of Africa.

inkwell, he leaned over and drew a line from pole to pole approximately three hundred miles west of the Azores and the Cape Verde Islands. All non-Christian lands east of this "Line of Demarcation" belonged to Portugal, declared the Holy Father, and all to the west belonged to Spain. Although Pope Alexander VI had made a good start, his decision did not settle the matter entirely. After discussions among themselves, in June 1494, the parties agreed to shift the line 1,100 miles west of the Cape Verdes.

Neither imagined that "the Line," as it came to be known, would influence history in so many ways. For example, Brazil, discovered in 1500, fell east of the line, into the Portuguese sector. Even today, when the Portuguese and Spanish empires have long-since vanished, the cultural effects of the Line persist. The peoples of Central and South America speak Spanish, except in Brazil, where people speak Portuguese.

Spaniards soon began to settle on their side of the Line. At first, that meant certain islands located in the Caribbean Sea. In 1502, they established their first permanent colony on La Isla Espaniola, or Hispaniola, "The Spanish Isle," shared today by Haiti and the Dominican Republic. Hispaniola and its neighbors—Cuba, Jamaica, Puerto Rico—belong to an island group known as the Greater Antilles. Named after the legendary Antilia, or Islands of the Seven Cities of Gold, these islands became stepping-stones to the Spanish Main.

Spain's colonies were never meant to exist on their own, much less govern themselves. They existed purely for the sake of the mother country and its rulers. No Spanish citizen could just pick up and go to the New World to live or trade. Before boarding a ship or loading a cargo, you had to obtain an official permit and a letter from a priest certifying that you were a good Catholic free of "false beliefs." Violators were punished according to their station in life. People of "gentle birth" paid heavy fines and faced banishment from Spain and her colonies for ten years. Those of "mean condition" spent eight years as slaves aboard a galley, a type of warship powered by oars and sails. Apart from a few minutes each day to visit a latrine, galley slaves stayed chained to their seats. Whipped to make them pull the heavy oars, few survived to the end of their sentences. The moment a slave died at his oar, guards pitched his body overboard and brought someone else to take his place.

Since merchants could not travel freely, and all imports were heavily taxed by the royal treasury, everything cost twenty to fifty times more in the colonies than in Europe. Colonists had no choice in the matter, for they could not produce everything they needed. Essential items like seeds, livestock, tools, cloth, glassware, paper, guns, and ammunition had to come from the mother country.

High prices created opportunity for non-Spaniards willing to live dangerously. Make no mistake about it: you took your life into your hands by venturing into the Spanish domain. Foreigners had no rights whatsoever in the New World. Not only did the government bar outsiders from colonial ports, it forbade their ships to cross the Line for any reason. Spanish law defined any unlicensed vessel captured in forbidden waters as a pirate craft and ordered everyone aboard hung on the spot. (This is the origin of the phrase "putting your life on the line.") Foreigners came anyhow. English, French, and Dutch smugglers brought their cargoes ashore at night. Eager to buy at "fair" prices, colonists took whatever they offered and asked for more. Government officials often looked the other way, also for a fair price.

The discovery of precious metals raised the stakes further. Spaniards said they came to the New World "to serve God and also to get rich." Serving God meant converting the natives to Christianity, thereby gaining spiritual treasure in Heaven and assuring themselves eternal life. Treasure on Earth, particularly gold, was equally important.

Oro, the Spanish word for gold, has a musical sound; *tesoro,* treasure, means a large amount of gold. Not only is this ancient symbol of wealth hard to come by, it always stays the same. Gold left at the bottom of the ocean for centuries shows no sign of decay; it is as bright as the day it went down. Better yet, gold could work "miracles." With enough of it, the poorest man might

This Aztec mask of gold was part of the treasure Hernán Cortés sent to Spain after his conquest of Mexico in 1521. Since the Aztecs sacrificed thousands of their people to the gods each year, skulls often appeared in their works of art.

remake himself as a *hidalgo,* short for *hijo de algo;* that is, a "son of someone" equal to the proudest nobleman. He could change his life by purchasing land, hiring people to work for him, and marrying a fine lady. Why, he could even use gold as a metallic passport to Heaven. "Gold is most excellent," explained Columbus in a letter of 1503 to King Ferdinand and Queen Isabella, because "he who has it does all he wants in the world, and can even lift souls up to Paradise."[1] Spaniards were not alone in their yearning for gold—far from it. All Europeans prized the yellow metal.

Between 1519 and 1532, bands of Spanish gold seekers led by Hernán Cortés and Francisco Pizarro overthrew the Aztec Empire in the Valley of Mexico and the Inca Empire in the Andes

Tolteca acalotli ypan ōcāmicovac.

This drawing from an Aztec manuscript shows Hernán Cortés leading his troops and the Indian allies in the attack on Mexico City.

Mountains of Peru. Although these empires had millions of subjects and their warriors vastly outnumbered the invaders, they were technologically backward. Native warriors fought on foot with stone-headed clubs, spears, and bows and arrows. These weapons were no match for the Spaniards' steel armor, crossbows, guns, and horses. Although horses had lived in the New World in prehistoric times, they died out about ten thousand years ago. The Spanish conquistadores, or conquerors, reintroduced them in the early 1500s. In their hands, *el caballo,* the horse, became a war-winning weapon. Small groups of armored cavalrymen crushed native armies like tanks rolling over blades of grass.

Native Americans lacked gunpowder and steel but had plenty of gold and silver. Unlike Europeans, who valued these metals as money, Native Americans admired them for their beauty as jewelry and used them in works of art. By 1650, Spaniards had found, looted, or mined an estimated 750,000 pounds of gold and 35.2 million pounds of silver, an amount worth at least ten billion dollars in today's money.

Gold did strange things to the invaders. The very idea of *oro* seemed to turn them into beasts lacking all self-control. They dreamed of gold, prayed for gold, worshiped gold as an idol. Seeing how Spaniards "longed and lusted for gold" shocked an Aztec chieftain. "Their bodies swelled with greed, and their hunger was ravenous; they hungered like pigs for that gold."[2]

The impact of conquest on the Indians has been compared to the Holocaust, the slaughter of European Jews by the Nazis during World War II. Not all Spaniards, of course, took part in the slaughter; the myth that they did is called *La Leyenda Negra,* the Black Legend. Some Spaniards, like Father Bartolomé de las Casas and Antonio de Montesinos, denounced the conquistadores to their faces, calling them un-Christian. Nevertheless, their words usually fell on deaf ears.

Forced labor and starvation, disease and outright murder, took a dreadful toll on native peoples. Smallpox and measles killed millions who had no natural immunity to these European diseases. "The Great Dying," as historians call this epic tragedy, created severe labor shortages, solved by creating yet another tragedy. The search for cheap labor sent hundreds of European slave traders to Africa each year. By 1600, they had brought 275,000 black people to the New World as slaves; five times that number would arrive during the next century. An equal number (at least) died on the "middle passage," the journey from Africa to America.[3]

Treasure bought Spaniards more than the good life—more, even, than a passport to paradise. It bought national power. Every year, sailors loaded chests of gold and silver bars into powerful

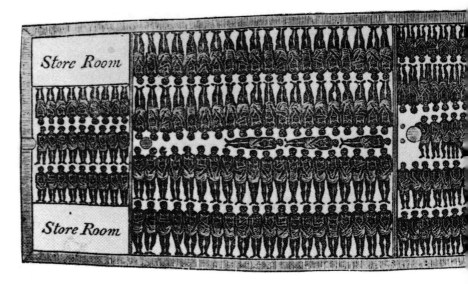

Diagram of the hold of a ship used in the African slave trade. Since space was scarce belowdecks, ship owners thought carefully about how to pack the most people into the available space.

warships called galleons for the voyage back to Spain. Upon reaching the port of Seville, the treasure underwent a miraculous transformation. Workers in the royal mint turned silver bars into pesos or "pieces of eight," each coin having the purchasing power of fifty dollars in today's money; gold coins, or "doubloons," were worth about two hundred dollars. His Majesty, the king, claimed 20 percent—the "Royal Fifth"—of all precious metals brought from the colonies. Once the royal share left the mint as coins, he used it to pay soldiers, build warships, and generally make Spain the most feared nation in Europe.[4] No, Europe's most *hated* nation.

Alarmed at Spain's growing power, in 1523, France protested in no uncertain terms. "I should like," said King Francis I, "to see the clause in Adam's will that excludes me from a share of the world."[5] This time, the pope refused to interfere. So, when Spain refused to share, he encouraged French seamen to trade illegally and seize Spanish treasure ships. It was simple justice, he felt, to steal from Spaniards what they had stolen from the Indians. Yet,

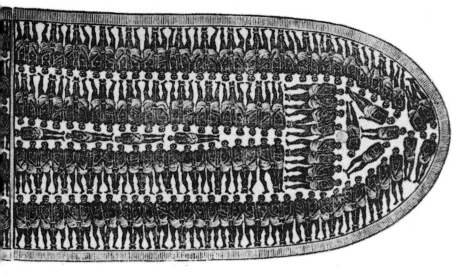

in Spanish eyes, these "corsairs" were criminals. King Francis, however, denied all knowledge of their activities, though he gladly took a share of the loot. The English and Dutch quickly followed his example.

Religion made matters worse. In 1517, a German monk named Martin Luther denounced the Roman Catholic Church as corrupt and irreligious. Luther's movement, Protestant Reformation, spread across Europe like wildfire. England and Holland turned Protestant. France stayed Catholic, but only after a series of bloody civil wars. Spain also remained Catholic, thanks largely to the Inquisition, a sort of religious secret police that executed anyone holding "heretical," or false, beliefs. Seeing themselves as defenders of the "true" religion, Spaniards aided other Catholic governments. Spanish agents tried to assassinate Protestant rulers and interfered in the French civil wars.

Europe's troubles spilled over into the New World. Protestant seamen swarmed across the Line to attack "Satan's darling,"

A drawing of Martin Luther with a dove and a halo, done about the year 1520. Luther created the religious split between Roman Catholics and Protestants, causing the wars of religion that ravaged Europe for more than a century.

Spain. Like the conquistadores, French Huguenots and Dutch Sea Beggars also wished to serve God and get rich. Yet, for courage and daring, none matched the Englishman Francis Drake. During the 1570s, he plundered shipping along the Spanish Main and seized a mule train loaded with treasure on a jungle trail in Panama. Drake had an uncanny ability to think like his opponents. Spaniards called him *el diablo negro,* "the black demon," claiming he used a crystal ball, given him by a witch, to find their ships on the high seas. Once located, no Spanish vessel ever escaped capture.

In later years, Drake raided cities along the coast of Spain itself, captured Spanish ships on the Pacific coast of South America, and sailed around the world aboard the *Golden Hind,* becoming the first Englishman to accomplish this awesome feat. In 1588, he played a leading role in the defeat of the "Invincible Armada," a huge fleet sent by the Spanish king Philip II, to conquer England.

Men like Drake could easily have ignited wars in the Old World. That they did not was due to an unwritten understanding among European governments. Rather than risk disaster over incidents thousands of miles from their shores, they agreed to this basic principle: "There is no peace beyond the Line." In short, they would not allow violence in America to disturb the peace of Europe. Adventurers might cross the Line whenever they pleased. If successful in robbing the Spaniards, good for them! Their actions changed nothing in Europe. If, however, the Spaniards caught them, their governments kept quiet and did nothing. Thus, the New World became a permanent war zone where the rules of normal relations between nations did not apply.

Sea raiders operated under handicaps of distance and time. Based in European home ports, they had to cross a treacherous ocean simply to reach their targets. Moreover, nearly every scrap of food, every piece of rope and sail canvas, every bucket of tar and keg of gunpowder, had to go aboard with them or be taken from the Spaniards by force. Clearly, shuttling back and forth across the Atlantic for supplies did not leave much time for "productive" work. There was only one thing to do: set up permanent bases on the Caribbean islands.

Although Spaniards had colonized the Greater Antilles, they had bypassed many smaller islands, among them a group called the Lesser Antilles. Nevertheless, Spain claimed these, too. It was

The worlds furuaied bounds, braue Drake on thee did gaze,
Both North and Southerne Poles, haue feene thy manly face.
If thanklefse men conceale, thy prayfe the starres woulde blaze,
The Sunne his fellow-trauellers worth will dueiy grace
Ro Vaudian fculp.

Boston. N.E. Published by S G Drake 1857.

In the late 1500s, Sir Francis Drake raided Spain's colonies in the New World, as well as Spain itself, in search of treasure and to avenge Spanish attacks on his fellow Englishmen. From a photograph of a drawing made in 1857.

enough for a captain just to see an island as his ship passed in the distance for it to become automatically a Spanish possession.

That was fine, as long as Spain had the power to enforce her claims. By the early 1600s, however, she had passed her prime. Too many wars had drained her treasury and stifled her industries with high taxes. She still claimed everything west of the Line, but the population of the islands was small and spread over an immense area. Her military men did not have enough ships to patrol all coastal waters all the time. Thus, each year found Spain less able to defend her far-flung possessions.

At the same time, Spain's rivals, sensing weakness, became bolder. Between 1623 and 1640, they "planted" tiny settlements on several unoccupied islands. Frenchmen settled Martinique and Guadeloupe. Dutchmen landed on Curaçao, Saba, and St. Eustatius; they also shared St. Martin with the English. The English shared St. Kitts with the French and occupied Barbados, Nevis, Antigua, and Montserrat on their own.

These settlements were not planted by governments, but by private investors hoping to profit from agriculture, illegal trade, and raiding—particularly raiding. In return for a share of the loot, island merchants supplied the raiders' needs. Likewise, island governors, sent out by the mother country, allowed raiders to repair their vessels in secluded bays and coves. Finally, in 1655, an English fleet captured Jamaica. This *was* different! For the first time, a foreign government had seized an island inhabited by Spaniards and set up its own colony.

The conquest of Jamaica gave Henry Morgan his big chance. Using Jamaica as a base of operations, Morgan launched devastating raids against Spanish possessions in the New World. Between 1668 and 1671, he attacked key cities in Cuba and present-day Venezuela, then went on to sack Panama City, the "treasure house" of the New World. These raids went a long way toward weakening the Spanish Empire, the greatest the world had seen since the days of ancient Rome.

Henry Morgan and Francis Drake would have understood each other perfectly. Like Drake, Morgan had boundless ambition and fantastic luck. He was the right man at the right time. Spain's growing weakness and his unique gifts for inspiring others to

A drawing of Sir Henry Morgan from an early English edition of John Esquemeling's book *The Buccaneers of America.*

work together enabled Morgan to rise from obscurity to lead the buccaneers.

People have long been fascinated by the buccaneers and their "cousins," the pirates. Legends in their own time, their exploits have given rise to countless tales of adventure and romance. In literature, the line from Daniel Defoe's fictional *Life, Adventures, and Piracies of the Famous Captain Singleton* to Robert Louis Stevenson's classic, *Treasure Island,* is at once clear and direct. Sea raiders have also figured in at least seventy films. Movie pirates have ranged from Errol Flynn as the swashbuckling Sea Hawk to Dustin Hoffman as the comical Hook. Another film, *The*

Black Swan, starring Tyrone Power, was based on the adventures of Morgan and his men.

But a word of caution is necessary when considering the buccaneer life. Fiction, particularly good fiction, can easily blur the difference between entertainment and truth. By playing to our emotions, fiction tempts us to identify with attractive figures, even glorify them. Yet, in the words of an old saying: "Romance is crime in the past tense." Real buccaneers were not romantic heroes. Their ranks included some of the most ferocious fighters ever to stride the heaving deck of a ship. How they got that way, and why, is anything but romantic.

One thing that will strike the reader, as it struck this author, is the ugly violence that prevailed in Sir Henry Morgan's day. People regarded violence in its various forms—war, torture, rape, looting—as normal and acceptable. Soldiers thought nothing of mistreating captives, and captives usually expected the worst. This was the era when Europeans fought wars over differing views of the Christian religion.

The wars' horrors, however, showed what awaited *everyone* unless they came to their senses and brought violence under control. Statesmen responded by devising a system of international law aimed not at abolishing war, but at limiting its savagery. By the time Sir Henry Morgan died in 1688, most people in Europe and its colonies knew it was a crime to harm civilians deliberately or kill enemy prisoners.

These rules have become part of our heritage as civilized people. Still, twentieth-century wars have often been as frightful as any fought in the seventeenth century. We need only think of the Holocaust, the massacres in Rwanda, and the horrors of Bosnia to see that savagery is still very much with us. But there is a difference between our world and Sir Henry Morgan's. Unlike the people of his time, today the world recognizes that certain actions are criminal, even in war, and deserve the harshest punishment. This shows that humanity can make progress, if slowly.

Sir Henry Morgan may not have been a likable person. We cannot be sure, since there are no written accounts of his private life, and he knew how to keep secrets. History remembers him as a thief, and so should we. Yet, to be fair, we must also remember that he was a product of his age, as we are of ours. Although circumstances change over time, the underlying human realities persist. Morgan's life touches upon themes familiar to us today: war, poverty, greed, crime, oppression, religious bigotry, racial prejudice, injustice. So, by picturing the buccaneer chief in his own time and place, we can experience enduring aspects of the human condition.

Everything known about Morgan suggests that he lacked any shred of generosity. Neither patriotism nor religion nor high moral principle seem to have guided his actions. His chief motive, perhaps his only motive, was to enrich himself—at other people's expense. In this he was far from unique. We need only recall the American "robber barons" of the 1890s to see that no person or age has a monopoly on selfishness; indeed, some robber barons proudly compared themselves to the old-time buccaneers. In their scramble for wealth, these bankers and industrialists may have been more sophisticated than Morgan. Whereas he took what he wanted by brute force, they used cutthroat competition, bribery, fraud, and political manipulation. Still, they shared the same goal as Morgan: to enrich Number One. That, of course, is a goal that is still shared by many people today.

Here is a paradox. If the robber barons caused terrible suffering (and they did), they also became agents of progress, serving ends larger than themselves. Ideas and actions often have unexpected results. Thus, without meaning to, the robber barons helped their country become the greatest economic and military power of all time. Similarly, Henry Morgan's exploits had consequences he never imagined. While pursuing his own interests, he unintentionally became a founder of the British Empire. And that concerns us in a very direct way, for eventually America and Britain used their power to save democratic nations—and democratic values—during two world wars. Building empires is not necessarily progress; cooperation and respect are also ways of achieving the advancement of humanity. However, historians must deal with historical fact; that is, the past as it was, not as it might have been.

Sir Henry Morgan was several men wrapped together into one. He was an adventurer and a colonial governor; a slave trader and a plantation owner; a country gentleman and a ruthless gambler; a self-made man and a tool of empire. As a soldier and sailor, he combined the imagination to dream "impossible" dreams and the ability to make them reality.

Old Harry did more than anyone else to break Spain's monopoly in the West Indies, erase the Line from the maps, and keep the islands for England. Today we can look back and see the story unfold to its "inevitable" conclusion. Yet, in the seventeenth century, all was suspense and uncertainty. Although the chief actor left the stage in 1688, we may still see his legacy in the fertile Jamaican valley where he owned a plantation. Morgan's Valley is approached through Morgan's Pass by way of Morgan's River and Morgan's Forest. Meanwhile, at Port Royal, guides proudly tell tourists about the bold buccaneer who used to walk those same streets.

One
A Passage to America

"Oh, England is a pleasant place for them that's rich and high.
But England is a cruel place for such poor folk as I."
—Charles Kingsley, *The Last Buccaneer*

"And surely the very hearing of these things could not but make
the weak to quake and tremble."
—William Bradford, *Of Plymouth Plantation, 1620–1647*

The future buccaneer's early years are virtually a complete blank, and three centuries of historical detective work have revealed little more than a few tidbits of information. All we know for certain is that he was born in 1635 in County Monmouth, Wales, a part of the British Isles ruled by the king of England. It is likely that his father was Robert Morgan, a farmer of the "middling sort"; that is, neither rich nor poor, but prosperous enough to work his land with the help of hired laborers. Nothing is known about the boy's mother or if, indeed, his parents were married.[1]

Henry once summarized his youth in a brief sentence. At the age of forty-five, he wrote: "I left school too young to be a great proficient in [learning], and have been much more used to the pike than the book."[2] Henry knew his own heart and mind. Nothing he ever did shows the slightest interest in the arts, religion, or ideas. That reference to the pike, however, reveals where his interests lay. The pike was a heavy spear, from fifteen to twenty feet long, used by soldiers before the invention of the bayonet. When formed into squares, masses of pikemen advanced with their weapons pointed straight ahead, ready to jab them into the enemy's faces. During cavalry charges, pikemen placed their weapons under the heel of one foot for support and pointed them at the chests of oncoming horses. Either way, "pike squares" could sweep across a battlefield like steel-quilled porcupines.

Henry lived in an age when war, not peace, was the normal condition. Seventeenth-century writers often defined peace as "the time betwixt wars." From 1618 to 1714, Europe seldom enjoyed more than a few years of peace in a row. War became as predictable as the change of seasons. Come spring, kings rolled out their artillery and set their forces in motion. At the first snowfall, fighting stopped and the fighters settled into winter quarters. In between, they fought for God, glory, territory, trade, and to avenge past wrongs. These, of course, aroused desires for further vengeance.

Conflicts lasted years, even decades. The Thirty Years' War (1618–1648), the worst ever, involved much of the European continent in a savage struggle between two branches of the Christian religion: Roman Catholicism and Protestantism. Earlier, during the Middle Ages, knights had observed a code of honor that respected enemies. They tried, if possible, not to kill an enemy, but to take him prisoner and hold him for ransom. All that changed during Henry Morgan's childhood. As Catholic and Protestant armies ran wild, artists portrayed the "Wolf War God" consuming everything in its path. Both sides routinely cut prisoners' throats.

A pikeman from the era of the **Thirty Years' War** holds his weapon in the "carry" position.

"Innocent bystanders" no longer existed. It became a rule of war never to leave a countryside or its inhabitants available for the enemy to use as supplies and reinforcements. The passing of an army meant total devastation and mass starvation. During the

This anonymous print dates from about the year 1630. Titled "Wolf War God," it depicts the Thirty Years' War as a gigantic wolf eating everyone and everything in sight.

Thirty Years' War, in the worst-hit areas, like central Germany, rats, dogs, and cats vanished into the cooking pots. Starvation often led to cannibalism; even mothers were accused of eating their children. Armies routinely used torture to deter the peasants from enlisting in the opposing army. A German writer described the "Swedish cocktail," a drink made of manure drippings poured down a peasant's throat. Soldiers baked people alive in bread ovens. Tormented beyond endurance, local people might band together to make war in self-defense. Civilians ambushed patrols,

Ifrael ex. Cum Priul. Reg.

A la fin ces Voleurs infames et perdus ,
Comme fruits malheureux a cet arbre pendus

Monstrent bien que le crime (horrible et noire engeance)
Est luy mesme instrument de honte et de vengeance ,

Et que cest le Destin des hommes vicieux
Desprouuer tost ou tard la iustice des Cieux . *1)*

killing every man, or murdered soldiers as they slept. In return, their comrades killed everyone they could lay their hands on.

The Morgan family played its part in this colossal tragedy. Young Henry's uncles, Edward and Thomas, fought on the Protestant side in the Netherlands and Germany. They served not as subjects of their king, who stayed neutral, but as soldiers of fortune, who fought for pay. Nobody saw anything wrong in this, because mercenaries followed an ancient and honorable profession. Europe had no military colleges in the seventeenth century. Since those interested in a military career could not get training if their country was at peace, they did the next best thing. Thousands enlisted in the army of a country at war; soldiers called it "following the wars." That did not mean that a volunteer agreed with a ruler's cause, only that he served to learn the soldier's trade. The boy's uncles were fast learners, both rising to the rank of colonel. We can imagine him listening in wonder to their adventures in foreign lands.

England, too, needed soldiers. In 1642, when Henry was

During the Thirty Years' War, each side often hanged prisoners. This engraving is by the French artist Jacques Callot and appeared in a book titled *Les Misères et les malheurs de la guerre (The Miseries and Tragedies of War)*, published in Paris in 1633.

seven, civil war exploded across the land. King Charles I and Parliament, the national legislature, fought when His Majesty raised taxes without the lawmakers' consent. As in other civil wars, the quarrel divided families and shattered friendships. The Morgan brothers were no exception. Edward joined the Cavaliers, or those who rallied to the king. Thomas joined the Roundheads, or the Parliamentary army; Roundheads wore their hair cut short in contrast to the long curls of their opponents. Described as "a little, shrill-voiced choleric man," Thomas caught the eye of Oliver Cromwell, the Roundhead leader, who promoted him to major general.[3]

An anonymous print showing the execution of King Charles I.

The Roundheads won several decisive victories. After capturing King Charles, in 1649 they beheaded him for treason before a vast crowd in London. Their leader gone, the Cavaliers' cause collapsed like a house of cards. Thousands fled to the continent, among them Edward Morgan, who married a German lady. With his brothers fighting on opposite sides of the English civil war, Henry's "father" played it safe by remaining neutral in word and deed. Robert Morgan's name does not appear in any court record, probably because he never got into trouble with the authorities.

The boy's life was as comfortable as anyone could expect in such troubled times. Still, Henry could not ignore the misery all around him. Part of that misery grew out of the civil war, inevitable when rival armies roam the countryside, drafting men and seizing supplies. Yet that was minor, compared to the ordinary, everyday struggle for survival. Misery was built into the social system, as much a reality as the ground Henry walked on and the air he breathed. Life for the majority was bleak, brutal, nasty—and short. Badly housed, badly clothed, and badly fed, most people had no hope of changing their situation in the country of their birth.

Through no fault of their own, Henry's countrymen fell victim to forces beyond their control. Spain's free-spending ways had caused a spectacular increase in the amount of gold and silver in circulation. This in turn led to a "price revolution." During the century after 1550, prices in Western Europe skyrocketed by at least 150 percent. As always, when things change, there are winners and losers. Landowners charged more for their crops and merchants' profits soared. Yet the majority—artisans, laborers, farmworkers—suffered because the cost of living rose faster than their wages. Although they normally worked sixteen hours a day, every year found them worse off than the year before. Life became pure drudgery, an endless battle just to keep their heads above water.

For us to see Henry's world through his eyes requires imagination. As landowners, the Morgan family would have lived in a stone-and-wood house furnished with sturdy oak tables and chairs, thick draperies, feather beds, and a fireplace in every room. For much of the year, those fireplaces made country life bearable. Italian and Spanish visitors constantly moaned about England's "thicke, cloudy, misty ayre," weeping skies, and raw, bone-chilling cold.[4] Wealthy people, too, struggled to keep warm, and the youngster must have had his share of chilblains and chapped lips.

A five-minute walk from his front door would have brought him to the farmworkers' homes. Entire families lived in tiny one-room cottages with thatch roofs. These, a traveler observed, "hath no other . . . hangings than what the spider affords, no other bed-steads, or table-boards, than the bare earth, no other bedding than strawe . . . no other couches, or chairs, or stooles, or . . . benches, or carpets, or cushions, than what nature hath wrought with her owne hands."[5]

Such dwellings were not for the weak or timid. Privacy did not exist, and children learned the facts of life early. The only fresh air came from gaps in the thatch roof, which leaked when it rained; windows were heavily taxed, and only families like Henry's could afford glass panes. Smoke from the cooking fire grew so thick that people's eyes watered and they developed hacking coughs. Cottages stank to high heaven. There was no escaping the foul odor, a blend of sweat, unwashed bodies, babies, and dirty linen. Since few workers could afford a change of clothes, they wore the same outfit year-round, usually without washing. If they did wash a garment, they passed it through a mixture of water and urine; the ammonia in the urine served as a bleach and disinfectant. Nor did they have a change of underwear. Worn until they fell to pieces, linen drawers harbored fleas and body lice, both carriers of disease.

In the towns, where most citizens lived in crowded slums, open sewers ran along both sides of the unpaved streets. Butchers killed animals in their shops and threw the refuse into the gutter. Garbage lay in heaps everywhere, perfect breeding grounds for vermin. Pigs roamed about freely, acting as scavengers. Residents, lacking toilets, emptied their wastes into the streets and allowed their children to go "filthing the streets."[6] Human wastes mingled with the soil and the daily deposits of horse manure. Rainstorms turned manure-filled streets into swamps of oozing brown muck. Summer breezes raised dust storms, blowing dried filth into citizens' faces and food. The odors became so unbearable that "delicate" ladies carried nosegays, little bunches of flowers, when venturing outdoors.

Putrid smells are signs of decay, and decay means germs. In our day, the typical elementary school pupil knows more about the causes of disease than the wisest person in Henry's time. Nobody in the seventeenth century knew that germs existed, let alone that they could make you sick. One accepted disease philosophically, as a normal danger of life, as we regard auto accidents. Few saw any need for cleanliness. Even royalty seldom washed. A few years before Henry's birth, the wife of a French king ordered the court perfumer to mix special scents; without them, she said, she could not go near her evil-smelling mate.

If you got sick, you would be wise to avoid the doctor. Frequently, he could do little good and much harm. Not only was he ignorant of the cause of disease, he knew little about the workings of the human body. Nobody understood that breathing carries oxygen to the lungs, or why, or that oxygen even exists. Nor did anyone understand the purpose of blood. Ignorant of the blood's chemistry, people thought it controlled character. For example, a "sanguine," or hot-blooded person, had a quick, fiery temper. A "phlegmatic," or cold-blooded person, had a dull, easygoing nature.

A visit to the doctor was enough to scare the bravest person, not to mention a child. Doctors favored three treatments: bleeding, purging, drugging. Bleeding meant drawing blood to allow harmful "vapors" to escape from the body. Purging "cleansed" the patient's insides by constant vomiting and enemas. Drugging involved various "medicines." For example, doctors treated fevers with two salted herrings slit down the back and tied to the soles of the patient's feet. For stomach ulcers, a medical textbook recommended a mixture of one part powdered crabs' eyes to four parts vinegar, swallowed at daybreak on an empty stomach. Another prescription contained dried toads, mouse droppings, gold dust, urine mixed with sugar, and parings from the patient's nails with boiled eels kept in a bag tied around his neck. Although certain herbal remedies may have worked, most "medicines" did more harm than good, and doctors always buried more patients than they cured.

The majority spent more than half their earnings on the "staff of life"—bread. Nearly all the rest went for rancid cheese and salt fish; few could afford meat more than twice a month. Since there were few charities, the poor had to get by on their own. Not everyone could. Passersby often saw the bodies of starvation victims lying along roadsides and in city streets. Death, therefore, would have been no stranger to young people.

The rich celebrated their good fortune by overeating and decorating their homes with paintings of food; a common theme is a cow's head on a platter surrounded by slabs of beef and coils of sausage. Although they ate more than the poor, rich people did not eat better, due to their ignorance of nutrition. A diet of fatty meats spiced with pepper or sweetened with honey, for example, is hardly a "balanced" diet. Thus, even those who could afford better food suffered from vitamin deficiencies. The sight of those with "deformed Bodies, crooked Legs and Feet, wry Necks" was only too common in Henry's time.[7] Disease and malnutrition killed two-thirds of all children before the age of four. Those who survived to adulthood seldom lived beyond the age of thirty-five.

Henry learned that the law was as deadly as any disease. Short of spending his life in a darkened room, he could not have avoided seeing the horrors of the legal system. God might take mercy upon sinners in the next world, but mercy had nothing to do with earthly justice. The boy lived in an exceptionally cruel age, the product of ignorance and insensitivity to suffering. Lacking any idea about reforming criminals, or of preventing crime by improving living conditions, his countrymen believed that only the severest penalties could discourage crime.

Minor offenses brought swift retribution. Henry, no doubt, saw gossips tied to stools and ducked in a pond until nearly drowned. Insulting another person brought a seat in the stocks, a wooden frame in which the head, hands, and legs were locked while onlookers threw rocks and filth. Serious offenses brought branding with a red-hot iron; cutting off the nose, ears, or a hand; blinding; and nailing the tongue to the stocks.

Nowadays, torture is outlawed by all civilized countries. In Henry's time, however, few questioned its justice and necessity. During criminal cases, called felonies, suspects underwent torture to extract information or a confession of guilt; torturers were professionals who passed their skills from father to son. There were no fewer than two hundred offenses for which convicted felons faced death. The crimes that most often carried the death penalty were murder, treason, highway robbery, burglary, arson, rape, and counterfeiting. One also faced execution for fishing in a nobleman's pond or stealing a silk handkerchief worth two shillings, about twenty-five cents in today's money.

The boy learned that death came in many forms. Hanging, the most common form, employed the gallows, two wooden uprights joined at the top by a crossbeam with a rope attached. Placing a ladder against the gallows, the executioner helped felons climb up, slipped the noose around their necks, and pushed them off. Since the drop did not always bring instant death, relatives and friends pulled on their legs to break their necks, putting them out of their misery.

Hanging was humane compared to hanging and quartering. In this frightful punishment, the executioner cut down his still-living victim, revived him, and then hacked him into four pieces. Finally, he stuck the pieces on long spikes set in the arches of a bridge or another public place. Felons might also be "broken at the wheel." Here the executioner tied the culprit to a wagon wheel set on a raised platform, then broke every bone in his body with an iron bar, leaving him to die slowly. Besides warning would-be felons of their fate, savage punishments served as mass entertainment. Citizens brought their children to jeer at the condemned and cheer the executioner.

Changes in the natural world triggered mass hysteria. Henry's neighbors, and probably he himself, gave a supernatural cause to anything that science could not explain. For example, eclipses of

the sun signaled God's anger, comets warned of coming disasters, and lightning bolts indicated the devil's presence. Even educated people believed that Satan's human servants, or witches, smeared their bodies with fat from murdered infants before flying on broomsticks and pitchforks to midnight "sabbaths," where they enjoyed un-Christian acts such as spitting on a crucifix and having sex with demons. Witches were supposed to brew thunderstorms, ruin crops, poison farm animals, suffocate infants in the cradle, and cause epidemics. Although anyone could be a witch,

A print by Jan Lukyea showing the burning of a Dutch witch in the late 1600s. Although witches were often strangled to spare them suffering, this poor woman was burned alive.

those who looked or acted different—the crippled, the insane, the retarded—were particularly suspect. Each year hundreds of terrified victims were hauled up the gallows or burned alive.

Seventeenth-century England and Wales had a population of 5.5 million. Although ten times that number live there comfortably today, in Henry's time the island seemed overpopulated. "The people," an observer wrote, "doe swarme in the land, as yong bees in a hive in June; insomuch that there is hardly roome for one man to live by another. The mightier like strong old bees thrust the weaker . . . out of their hives."[8] The writer had a point; there *were* too many people and too few jobs.

Landowners often found it more profitable to raise sheep than grow crops. Since a shepherd and his dog could look after an entire flock, unemployment among farmworkers soared. Unable to support themselves, thousands became homeless each year. Had Henry's father taken him to any town, they would have passed groups of hungry, ragged people wandering the roads, sleeping in fields, or digging for edible roots. In town, swarms of beggars waited outside churches and followed citizens from the moment they left their houses. When they became too pesky, town councils ordered them whipped through the streets and expelled. Hounded from place to place, the homeless formed gangs to terrorize neighborhoods, until the executioner caught up to them. Gangs frequently included children. When captured, those as young as nine died for stealing a loaf of bread or pickpocketing a silk handkerchief.

People started working earlier than they do nowadays. Sons of the wealthy acted as magistrates and government officials by their mid-teens. Boys of eleven and twelve, the sons of army or navy officers, accompanied their fathers to the wars. Poor children had few choices, none of them pleasant. There were no laws against child abuse, and parents could do as they pleased with their offspring. Normally, poor parents forced youngsters to leave home by the age of ten or twelve, but often at five or six. Unskilled and alone, these child throwaways survived as best they could in a dangerous world. Boys and girls helped on farms, dug ditches, and carried loads. In coal-rich Wales, children went into the mines, not to see daylight for days on end. The rest lost themselves amid the "great flockes of Chyldren" that trudged the roads or joined gangs.[9] Eventually, some reached the coastal towns, gateways to the sea and the New World beyond.

Henry Morgan also took to the road. Although he never gave a reason for leaving home, it could not have been for want of material things. His "poverty" must have been internal, a longing felt in his heart and soul. Judging from his later career, he had an adventurous spirit, one that wanted more from life than the safety of his father's house.

We may imagine him years later, nodding in agreement over the diary of Edward Barlow, another farmer's son, who went to sea at seventeen. "I never had any great mind to country work, as ploughing and sowing and making hay and reaping, nor also of winter work, as hedging and ditching and thrashing and dunging amongst cattle, and suchlike drudgery," Barlow wrote in his journal. He pitied his neighbors—fine, upstanding folks but without curiosity or courage. "Some of them would not venture a day's journey from out of the [sight of the] smoke of their chimneys or the taste of their mother's milk, not even upon the condition that they might eat and drink of as good cheer as the best

Nova Britannia.

OFFERING MOST

Excellent fruites by Planting in
VIRGINIA.

Exciting all such as be well affected
to further the same.

LONDON

Printed for SAMVEL MACHAM, and are to be sold at
his Shop in Pauls Church-yard, at the
Signe of the Bul-head.
I 6 o 9.

Title page of a pamphlet advertising the opportunities awaiting those lucky English people who decide to settle in Virginia.

nobleman in the land, but would rather stay at home and eat a little brown crust and a little whey."[10]

The colonies needed people. The early English settlers of Virginia and the West Indies were usually men of means, able to cross the Atlantic at their own expense. Yet, like the Spaniards before them, they faced severe labor shortages. There were simply not enough hands to build houses, clear the land, and plant the chief cash crops: tobacco, cotton, sugar, ginger, and indigo, valued for its blue dye. Planters, therefore, imported enslaved people from Africa. In addition, they hired agents to recruit English workers. Master showmen, these agents deluged the country with letters and pamphlets supposedly written by happy colonists. Comparing the colonies to paradise on Earth, they promised high adventure, full bellies, and easy living under sunny skies. It worked. In the words of a popular song of the time, thousands reached for "The Pie in the Sky."

So did Henry Morgan. Sometime in 1654, the nineteen-year-old tied some clothes into a bundle, slung it over his shoulder, and set out for the coast. As he paced off the miles, it must have felt as if he had turned his back on everything familiar. Gradually, the Welsh uplands gave way to the low, rolling countryside of western England. No longer did the wind carry the scent of woods and fields, but of saltwater and tar. Ahead lay Bristol, the country's busiest seaport, second only to the capital, London.

Henry rented a room in one of the inns lining the muddy

streets leading to the waterfront. Standing at the front door, he could see hundreds of ships moored side by side, three and four deep. Walking toward them, he passed a jumble of taverns, wharves, warehouses, wooden cranes, timber yards, supply sheds, and sailmakers' lofts.

A gallows stood at the end of a stone jetty, positioned so as to make the swaying body of a pirate visible from the ships. Piracy was nothing new in Henry's day. Seafaring and sea roving had always gone together. Pirates—the word comes from *peiran*, Greek for "to take"—were deemed enemies of the human race, because they attacked any and all vessels, including those of their own nations. An old English law defined them as villains "with whom neither Faith or Oath is to be kept," but treated as *"Brutes and Beasts of Prey."*[11] Capture meant certain death. Most pirates were simply hung and their bodies tossed into unmarked graves. Notorious pirates, however, got special treatment. Their bodies were covered with tar to preserve them, wrapped in chains, and hung in a public place, where they remained for years as examples to others.

Bristol's waterfront worked its magic. A kaleidoscope of humanity presented itself at every turn, gesturing with gnarled hands and babbling in strange tongues. Henry saw red-faced Dutchmen rolling barrels of pickled herrings and olive-skinned Italians selling spices brought overland by camel from the Indian Ocean to Constantinople on the Mediterranean Sea. He rubbed shoulders with swarthy Frenchmen bringing wine from Burgundy and blond Norwegians off North Sea whaling ships. The youngster marveled at Englishmen returning from the West Indies with parrots and monkeys perched on their shoulders. Now and then he passed a broken-down old sailor, crippled by some accident, begging "your worship" for a few pennies.

An unnamed pirate hanged at dockside. Notice that he did not fall through a trapdoor, which would have broken his neck instantly and painlessly. He was pushed off the end of a cart, causing slow strangulation. Someone placed a bouquet of flowers in his hands to "sweeten" his last moments on Earth.

Although seamen differed in nationality, Henry found that they had more in common with each other than with landsmen of the same country. To begin with, they dressed differently: Sailors wore short canvas jackets over checked shirts and baggy trousers coated with tar for insulation against cold and damp. They tied scarves around their necks and wore woolen caps on their heads. Except while ashore, they went barefoot so that the soles of their feet became hard and rough. Going barefoot provided a firmer grip on slippery decks than wearing shoes did.

Henry learned that the British sailor called himself "Jack Tar," slang for a man (jack) who always smelled of tar. As one of society's castoffs, the typical Jack Tar had shipped out in his late teens or early twenties; his average age was twenty-seven. Usually a small, wiry fellow of between 120 and 140 pounds, he was agile as a cat, which made him ideal for climbing rope ladders and working on yardarms, the crosspieces on the masts from which the sails hung. Months of walking on a rolling deck made Jack Tar sway from side to side to keep his balance, yet he trod firmly "where all other creatures tumble."[12]

Years of exposure to the elements had darkened Jack Tar's skin, giving it a coarse, wrinkled look. Tattoos adorned his body. He made the designs himself, or had a friend do it, by puncturing the skin with a needle and rubbing in gunpowder or ink. Even ships' boys, children hired to do odd jobs, had tattoos. A boy named Jeoly, for example, "was painted [tattooed] all down the Breast, between his Shoulders behind; on his Thighs (mostly) before; and in the Form of several broad Rings, or Bracelets round his Arms and Legs."[13]

It could not have taken long for Henry to realize that Bristol was a great deal more than a seaport; it was also a gigantic flesh market. Wise men looked the other way whenever a warship of the Royal Navy anchored in the harbor.

Heavy battle losses and harsh living conditions gave the navy a dreadful reputation. So a captain who needed men to complete his crew would have waited forever for volunteers. Instead, he re-sorted to "impressment," a polite term for legalized kidnapping. No man or boy was safe. You could be walking down the street, or leaving church, when a band of sailors called a "press gang" clubbed you to the ground. Next thing you knew, you awoke aboard their ship with a splitting headache and a warning to obey orders—or else. If you were the family breadwinner, and your loved ones starved in your absence, that was too bad. Nothing they said or did could bring you back.

Not everyone who passed through Bristol did so willingly. Rather than hang wrongdoers or pay for their upkeep in jail, the government turned the colonies into a dumping ground for soci-ety's castoffs. "Certainly," one writer noted, "these islands must be the very scum of scums, the mere dregs of corruption."[14] Al-most every day, weather permitting, Henry would have seen guards driving batches of chained beggars, criminals, and war prisoners aboard the ships. Upon arriving in Virginia or the West Indies, ship captains auctioned this so-called "human rubbish" to the highest bidder.

Flesh merchants roamed the streets of Bristol. Most danger-ous were the "spirits," dealers in stolen children, usually home-less children, but any child they could snatch and sell to a ship's captain was fair game. Kidnapping was big business in the 1600s. One spirit took an average of 500 children a year over a period of twenty years; another boasted of taking 850 children in a single year. Spirits also bought children from poverty-stricken parents.

Since most poor children could neither read nor write, they left no record of their ordeals. Richard Frethorne was an excep-tion. He wrote his parents from Virginia: "It is most pitifull if you did knowe as much as I, when people crie out day and night, Oh that they . . . would not care to lose anie lymbe [limb] to be in England againe. . . . If you love me, redeem me and let me come home. O that you did see my daylie and hourelie sighs, grones, and teares. . . . I thought no head had been able to hold so much water as hath and doth daylie flow from mine eyes."[15] If they replied, we have no record of it.

The majority of people, however, sold themselves into servitude. To pay their passage, these "free-willers" signed an indenture, or contract, agreeing to work on a plantation for three to seven years. During this time the master had to provide them with food, clothing, and shelter. In certain cases, he promised to give a few acres of farmland, seeds, and tools when the indenture expired.

How did Henry Morgan make his passage to America? Was he kidnapped? Did he sign an indenture? Did he pay his own way? Perhaps he shipped out as a seaman, or as a soldier with a military expedition. What was the voyage like? It is impossible to answer these questions with certainty, since there is no evidence either way. Still, we are not at a total loss. Countless others who made the crossing described their experiences in letters and diaries. Through their writings, and with a little imagination, we can join them on a "typical" Atlantic crossing. Although our voyage never took place exactly as described, it has elements in common with *every* seventeenth-century voyage.[16]

Those who boarded a seventeenth-century sailing ship for the first time often described the experience as stepping into a "wooden world." They did not exaggerate. Apart from a few metal fittings and the rope and canvas of the rigging, everything was made of wood. The most important parts of a sailing ship—its hull, decks, and masts—were made of seasoned oak. Not only could timbers be cut and shaped, they swelled when wet, allowing them to fit together tightly. This explains why sailors scrubbed the decks and doused them with buckets of saltwater at least once a day, and five times a day in the tropics. Washing, or "holystoning," had little to do with cleanliness; without constant soaking, the planks would shrink and crack. To keep the masts and yardarms from drying out, sailors rubbed them with fish oil.

Ocean-going vessels had two or three masts and were seventy to one hundred feet long by twenty-five feet wide. The thickness of their outer walls measured anywhere from fifteen inches for merchant vessels to forty inches for warships. Men-of-war (ships built only to fight, not to carry trade goods) needed thicker sides, because they had to withstand cannonballs.

Preparing for a voyage was difficult and time-consuming. Before anything else came aboard, dockworkers piled tons of sand on the ship's floor; that is, the lowest part of the frame, nearest the water. This additional weight, or ballast, gave the vessel stability, preventing it from riding too high and tipping over in rough seas. Next came the cargo and provisions, a bewildering array of boxes, barrels, bales, and bundles stowed in the holds. In addition, cattle, sheep, pigs, goats, and chickens were kept in pens belowdecks. Lacking refrigeration, an invention of the late 1800s, the only way to preserve meat was to salt it or to slaughter animals as needed.

Sailing day. Everyone not working belowdecks gathered topside to witness the spectacle of departure. At the captain's order, a trumpeter gave the signal. Instantly, as if by magic, the ship sprang to life. Brawny sailors rushed to the capstan, a wheel for

A warship of the mid-1500s. The picture is from a print based on a painting by the Belgian artist Pieter Brueghel the Elder.

lifting heavy cargo and raising anchors. Grabbing its wooden handles, they slowly turned it together. A big fellow set the pace with a shanty or work song. He began with a single line of verse, and before he spoke the last word the others sang the chorus. They sang "The Maid of Amsterdam," the most famous sea-song of all time:

In Amsterdam there dwelt a maid
Mark well what I do say;
In Amsterdam there dwelt a maid,
Her cheeks was red, her eyes was brown,
Her hair like glow-worms hanging down.
And I'll go no more a-roving
With you fair maid
A-roving, a-roving
Since roving's been my ru-i-n
I'll go no more a-roving
With you, fair maid.

With chains rattling up through the hawseholes, anchors rose from the muddy bottom as deckhands untied the cables holding the ship to the dock. Meanwhile, other crewmen climbed rope ladders to the yardarms and began to unfurl the sails. *Shush, shush, shush, shush.* The sound of rustling canvas gave way to a loud *snap* as acres of white sail caught the breeze.

The jolt kicked the vessel into motion. Slowly it pulled away from the dock, turned, and headed down the Bristol Channel.

Hours passed. The water became choppy. Winds blew fine spray into men's faces. The ship bobbed and dipped in the swells. Those standing on its port, or left, side noticed a long finger of land grow dim in the mist, then fade away. Jack Tars nodded to each other silently, knowingly. They had nothing to say, no words to express their feelings at that moment. Land's End, England's southernmost tip, now lay behind them. Before them stretched the Atlantic Ocean.

Deckhands work the capstan bars to raise their ship's anchor.

HORUSCE en HAREADEN BARBAROSSA

The Barbarossa
(Red Beard) brothers,
Muslim sea rovers
from North Africa,
terrorized the coasts
of England and
France. From a copy
of a French print
of the 1600s.

Lookouts stood in the crows' nests aloft, scanning the horizon
for other vessels. Only those men with the keenest vision could
serve as lookouts, and never for more than an hour or two at a
time, owing to the sun's glare. Belowdecks, gun crews prepared to
shoot first and ask questions later. You could never be too careful,
because the seas bordering Europe swarmed with pirates. The
majority were Europeans themselves—English, French, Dutch,
Irish, Spanish, Portuguese—based in secluded creeks and inlets.

Although savage fighters, they seemed tame alongside the pirates from Algiers, Tunis, and Salé in North Africa. Using swift, oar-powered galleys, these Muslim pirates captured hundreds of Christian vessels each year, often within sight of their home ports. Crewmen who resisted were butchered without mercy; the rest became galley slaves. Coastal villages also suffered. No villager could go to bed at night and be sure of awaking a free person, or walk along the shore without fear of being snatched by a landing party. Each year hundreds of Englishwomen and children wound up in North African slave markets.

After a few days on the open ocean, the crews settled into their routines. Henry soon learned that a ship was like a living creature, each part having its own role to perform on behalf of the whole organism. Officers were its brain. The captain commanded the ship; since he might also be an owner, he had a special interest in keeping things running smoothly. His mate, or second in command, handed out the work assignments and served as navigator.

The seventeenth-century navigator used several instruments to shape a course and keep to it. His compass, a large magnetized needle fastened to a card, gave the ship's direction at all times. At night, he used a cross staff to find the ship's position in relation to the North Star. By day, the navigator measured the sun's angle to the horizon with an astrolabe and a quadrant. Both instruments helped in calculating latitude, the ship's position on the imaginary lines that circle the Earth north and south of the equator. Only the invention of the chronometer in the late 1700s enabled navigators to find a ship's longitude, or position east or west on the globe.

Sailors were the ship's muscles and limbs. Except in emer-

A seventeenth-century compass card. Although this example lacks the magnetized needle, it shows all the directions. The "crown" points true north.

gencies, when everyone lent a hand, they worked set watches, or tours of duty. A watch schedule was four hours on, then four hours off, and so on around the clock. A ship's boy timed the watches with a half-hour sandglass.

Experts at various trades kept the ship shipshape. The boatswain—bos'n for short—saw to the anchors, cables, sails, and rigging. Working under him, the sailmaker mended the sails and repaired their ropes. The carpenter took charge of the masts and decks. The cooper looked after the barrels containing water and provisions. The caulker tended to the pumps and sealed leaks in the hull by hammering in wooden plugs or forcing oakum, shredded rope impregnated with tar, between the seams of the planks. The gunner cared for the weapons and ammunition, aided by his powder monkeys. During a battle, these boys supplied the gun crews with gunpowder from the magazine or ammunition storage room.

Topmen worked aloft. No vessel could maintain its speed or stay on course without their constant attention. From the main deck, topmen climbed the rigging until their comrades below appeared as small as dolls. Once aloft, they stood on tiny platforms that swayed over the water with every lurch and roll of the ship. From there they stepped out along the yardarms, holding on with their hands and balancing on footropes like high-wire artists performing without safety nets.

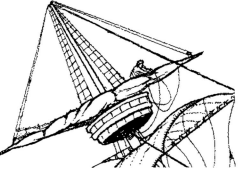

Each sail had about twelve ropes attached to it. The topmen controlled the sails by holding, pulling, or letting out these ropes. Every change in wind speed or direction sent them aloft to change the height or angle of the sails. In light breezes,

A topman leans out of a crow's nest to take in, or furl, a sail.

when the ship ran on an "even keel," they enjoyed standing on the footropes and swaying in time to the gentle rhythm. If the wind died down, they had to put out every stitch of canvas.

It was different in rough weather. When a gale blew, the sea rose in all its fury. At such times, the helmsman needed every ounce of his strength just to keep the ship moving in a straight line. She lurched forward, her planks groaning, plunging her bow under mountainous waves. Hissing water swept the length of the deck, forcing crewmen to hang on for dear life. Any false step pitched you overboard to certain death; it was impossible to slow the ship down or come about for a rescue. In an average storm, topmen lowered some sails, for otherwise the wind would bend the masts so far forward as to snap them off. In severe storms they furled all the sails to avoid capsizing. Occasionally sailors, suspecting witchcraft, killed a passenger and threw the body overboard in hopes of calming the raging sea.

If they were lucky, sailors worked in daylight. Everyone dreaded those pitch-black nights when the rain fell in sheets and the wind shrieked in the shrouds, the ropes that kept the masts steady. Edward Barlow described his experiences as follows:

> . . . at night when we went to take our rest, we were not to lie still above four hours; and many times when [a gale] blew hard were not sure to lie one hour, yea, often [we] were called up before we had slept half an hour and forced to go up into the maintop or foretop to take in our topsails, half awake and half asleep, with one shoe on and the other off, not having time to put it on: always sleeping in our clothes for readiness; and in stormy weather, when the ship rolled and tumbled as though some great millstone were rolling up one hill and

down another, we had much ado to hold ourselves fast by the small ropes from falling by the board [overboard]; and being gotten up into the tops, there we must haul and pull to make fast the sail, seeing nothing but air above us and water beneath us, and that so raging as though every wave would make a grave for us: and many times in nights so dark that we could not see one another, and blowing so hard that we could not hear one another speak, being close to one another; and thundering and lightening [lightning] as though Heaven and Earth would come together . . . with showers of rain so hard that it will wet a man "dunge wet" before he can go the length of the ship.[17]

Living conditions differed from those on modern ships. Today's travelers expect comfortable private cabins. In Henry Morgan's day, however, only the captain and officers had their own cabins in the ship's stern, its high rear section. Paying passengers squeezed into stuffy compartments "without enough space to swing a cat." An entire family, even strangers of both sexes, might share the same bed. Common seamen slept in the steerage, or the forward part of the hold. They had little space to move around, the headroom between decks seldom being more than five and one half feet, often less. Instead of beds, sailors slept in hammocks, a device borrowed from the Arawak people of the West Indies. Suspended on hooks driven into the ceiling, hammocks swayed and bounced with the ship's every motion. Indentured servants and convicts slept on the bare decks, with or without a blanket. "Comfort," however, was a relative term. During storms, pounding waves and windblown spray forced everyone to live in wet clothes.

An old rule governed life aboard ship: "Serve God daily, love one another, preserve your victuals, and beware of fire." Simply put and easily remembered, this rule grew out of centuries of experience at sea. Every phrase had meaning, and deserves to be explored in detail.

Nowhere did men feel so weak and insignificant as on the open ocean. Out there, their lives depended upon forces beyond human control. God ruled the deep in puzzling ways. He becalmed ships, allowing their crews to starve slowly, or drowned them quickly amid storm-tossed wreckage. To keep God's favor, most captains held prayer services at sunrise and sunset. This was a serious, almost grim, occasion. Disrespect during services threatened Divine vengeance upon everyone aboard. For that reason, culprits had to be punished before the entire company. The Royal Navy, for example, ordered them tied to the mainmast with a heavy iron spike "clapt cloese into their mouth and tyd behind their heads, and there to stand a whole houre, till their mouths are very bloody."[18]

Loving one another meant being a loyal shipmate. Survival depended upon fair play. Dishonesty bred distrust, weakening the crew's unity and ultimately its ability to resist the common enemy, the sea.

Offenders came before the captain, a meeting to make the toughest character cringe. "A Captain," one sailor wrote, "is like a King at Sea, and his Authority is over all that are in his Possession."[19] Note the language: all aboard are in his possession—are, in fact, his property throughout the voyage. The captain ruled with an iron hand. Backed *by* the law, his word *was* law aboard his ship. No one could protest his rules or appeal his decisions. Like God, he could spare your life or take it as he pleased.

Shipboard discipline was not as cruel as the sentences handed out by judges ashore. We have no record of captains burning culprits alive or breaking them at the wheel. Nevertheless, none of the laws that protect sailors today existed until the mid-1800s.

Discipline was both harsh and degrading, however. It began with the "starter," a thick piece of rope, about a foot in length, with a double knot at the end. Whenever an officer noticed a seaman who needed speeding up, he shouted, "Start that man!" The nearest enforcer, usually the boatswain or his mate, whacked the laggard across the shoulders. Just a blow or two did the job; the poor fellow moved faster, and the beating stopped at once.

Captains could be devilishly cruel. Monday was called "market day," the day set aside for punishment. First thing in the morning, the boatswain's whistle summoned the crew to the mainmast to hear the offenders' names read out and learn the captain's sentences. Those guilty of ordinary offenses—fighting, stealing, laziness, insubordination—went to the bilboes, a seagoing version of the stocks. Repeat offenders were put in irons—chained—and kept in the darkest, wettest, dirtiest, smelliest place on the lowest deck. There they lived for a week on bread and water, amid swarms of rats and cockroaches.

A boatswain's mate using a length of rope to whip a sailor tied to the ship's shrouds. The style of the boatswain's hat indicates that this picture was drawn in the early 1700s.

Whipping was the most common punishment. With their shipmates looking on, offenders were stripped to the waist and their hands tied to the shrouds or capstan. Then the boatswain raised his cat-o'-nine-tails, a whip with nine strands of rope knotted at the ends. A single blow from the "cat" could knock a man down, leaving him breathless; several blows made his back look like raw hamburger. Afterward, the ship's surgeon doused it with saltwater, partly to increase the pain, partly to cleanse the wounds. Some men recovered after two hundred lashes, apparently no worse for the experience. Not everyone, however, survived or remained himself. Finding the pain unbearable, some men died of shock or lost their minds after thirty strokes.

Captains also had sailors hoisted to a yardarm with a rope around the waist, "and from thence . . . violently let fall into the sea, sometimes three several times, one after another; and if the offence be very foul, he is also drawn under the keel of the ship, which is termed keel-raking." Killing a fellow crewman or attacking an officer carried an automatic death penalty. Yet seamen never died; "death" seemed too harsh a word for them. Instead of dying, they "came to port," "struck their colors," or were "boarded by the grim reaper."[20]

Preserving victuals meant saving food, essential on long voyages. Sailors ate two meals a day, in midmorning and at midafternoon. The cook prepared each meal on the main deck over a fire built in a low-sided box filled with sand. "Belly timber" consisted of meat, fish, biscuit, and cheese. After butchering all the live animals, crews ate meat and fish preserved in barrels filled with salt or brine. A barrel, however, often contained "salt junk," pieces of tough, stringy flesh mixed with fat and bones. Biscuit was a type of bread made of flour and water. Baked rock-hard, like today's dog biscuits, "this bread did fetch the skin off the men's mouths."[21] Often it housed scores of hopping, crawling, squirming creatures; sailors preferred eating biscuit in the dark, so as not to see what was going into their mouths. Cheese, when not fuzzy with mold, might be so hard that sailors carved it into buttons rather than risk breaking their "grinders." Since water quickly spoiled in barrels, it was best to hold your nose while drinking the putrid stuff. "A sailor's stomach," veterans said, "could near digest iron." It had to if he hoped to stay alive.

Relief came from the beer bottle. In Henry Morgan's day, Europeans considered beer a necessity. Brewed from barley and hops, it was nutritious and therefore a regular part of the diet. Regardless of age or sex, everyone drank, including children; mothers used the ends of cloths moistened in beer to relieve infants' teething pains. Soldiers received two gallons a day, sailors one gallon. Beer warmed them against the damp cold, allowing them to forget the boredom and hardship of their lives, at least for a short time. Drunkenness aboard ship, however, earned twenty licks from the cat.

Preventing fire was as important as food and drink. "Sailing vessel" and "firetrap" meant the same thing. Fire was an ever-present danger. Edward Barlow put it this way:

Neither are ships and we poor seamen out of great danger of our lives in calms and fairest weather, for the least fire may set a ship on fire, many ships having been burnt by some careless man in smoking a pipe of tobacco; and in carelessless of the cook in not putting the fire well out at night; and of burning of a candle in a man's cabin, he falling asleep and forgetting to put it out . . . and in many other ways a ship is set alight, and when they are on fire, it is a hundred to one if that you put it out, everything being so pitchy and tarry that the least fire setteth it all in a flame; and also there is great danger of the [gun]powder, for the least spark with a hammer or anything else in the room where it is, or the snuff of a candle causeth all to be turned into a blast, and in a moment no hopes of any person's lives being saved from death in the twinkling of an eye.[22]

No precaution was too small to avoid such a calamity. Fire-fighting methods, however, were very simple. This advice, found in an old set of sailing instructions, is typical: "the . . . Captain [should] cause 2 hogsheads [large barrels] to be cut asunder in the midst and chained to the side; the soldiers and marriners to piss in them that they may always be full of Urin; to quench fire . . . [keep] 2 or 3 pieces of old sail ready to wet in the piss, and always cast it on the fire . . . as need shall require."[23] Although not very sanitary, the chemicals in urine make it an excellent fire retardant.

Shipboard sanitation, like sanitation ashore, hardly existed. Officers, crew, passengers: all lived in filth and stank to high heaven. No one washed, unless caught in a downpour, since freshwater was too scarce to use on the body; besides, sailors were never issued soap. Nor were there any toilet facilities as we understand them today. Weather permitting, when nature called you made your way to the "head" located at the ship's head end, or bow. There you found the "necessary seats" or "seats of ease-ment," rough planks with circular holes slung over either side. Holding on for dear life, swaying "between wind and waves," you relieved yourself as best you could, in front of anyone who cared to look, male and female. Toilet paper might be a page torn from a discarded book or the tarred end of a rope, shared by all. In stormy weather, you used any space you could find be-lowdecks.

Filth accumulated. Odors of dirt and decay filled the ship. Vermin multiplied. Cockroaches, lice, and fleas were annoying pests. Rats threatened your life by gnawing through provision barrels in the hold. As if that were not bad enough, they fell into water barrels, drowned, and left their bodies to poison the water. Sometimes these rodents destroyed so much food that the crew and passengers began to starve.

Starvation brought out the best and the worst in people. Some gave their last morsel to those hungrier than themselves. Others seized the opportunity to make money. One eyewitness reported, "Women and children made dismal cries and grievous complaints. The infinite number of rats that all the voyage had been our plague, we were now glad to make our prey and feed on; and as they were insnared and taken, a well grown rat was sold for sixteen shillings as a market rate. Nay, before the voyage did end . . . a woman great with child offered twenty shillings for a rat, which the proprietor refusing, the woman died."[24]

Henry Morgan may or may not have eaten roasted rat. We can be certain, however, that he suffered along with his fellow "landlubbers." Until you gained your "sea legs," life aboard ship gave a good imitation of hell. Crowded, dirty, and hungry, passengers went in terror of storms. Through the ship's sides they heard the waves crashing and the wind howling. The ship's risings and plungings flung them around, causing bruises and broken bones. The constant rocking brought seasickness some compared to "a slow death in a wet hell." Yet many held on through sheer willpower. One devoted clergyman ministered to his flock despite "making wild vomits into the black night."[25]

These experiences built fortitude, forcing people to accept things and do things they had never thought possible. This was especially true of women, supposedly the "gentle" sex. Men marveled at their courage and tenacity in the face of hardship. "You see weakly Women," one observed, "whose hearts have trembled to set foote in a Boate, but now imboldened to venter [venture] throogh these tempestuous Seas with their young Babes, whom they nurture up with their Breasts, while their Bodies are tossed on the trembling Waves."[26]

Henry must have known that few vessels crossed the Atlantic free of disease. At sea, as on land, people faced the same killers: bubonic plague, typhus, smallpox, food poisoning, and scurvy, caused by a lack of the vitamin C that is found in fruits and vegetables. The ship's surgeon could set broken bones well enough, but when it came to fighting disease, he was as helpless as his counterparts ashore. Thus, a passenger wrote, "our Shipp was so full of infection that after a while we saw little but throwing folks over boord."[27]

Jack Tar never went off duty entirely; he always had something to do or check on. Serving as both teacher and worker, he trained the new men on the job. Aliens in the wooden world, these "greenhorns" had plenty to learn. Old-timers explained the differences between stem and stern; foremasts, mainmasts, and mizzenmasts; cat-harpins and belaying pins. Greenhorns had to "learn the ropes"—literally. Since handling the sails required different knots for different purposes, making a Flemish eye, a sheepshank, a timber hitch, and a diamond knot had to become second nature, something you could do automatically.

Jack Tar's vocabulary, however, was the hardest thing to learn. Sailors filled their speech with bewildering terms. What did they mean by "bunting the slack of the clews"? How did you "haul your bunt well up on the yard"? Why must you "have a care of the lee-latch"? What *was* a lee-latch? The youngster looked and listened, and learned.

Henry found that seamen had a unique sensitivity to their environment. They had built up an accurate body of knowledge about their surroundings, passed down by word of mouth over the centuries. Although they did not understand the science behind natural signs, they did understand their practical effects. For example, sailors knew that a bright moon means good weather, but that a halo around the moon signals a storm, as do red clouds on the horizon at sunrise or sunset.

These "sea scientists" were also superstitious. Sailors told tales of monsters uglier and more frightening than any nightmare. A ship-eating creature called the kraken (possibly the giant squid) lay on the ocean floor until forced to the surface by the fires of hell. Mile-long snakes coiled around vessels, crushing them instantly

and swallowing the survivors headfirst. Mermaids and mermen, creatures with the head and body of a human and the tail of a fish, lured mariners to watery graves. Ghost ships roamed the seas for eternity, doomed never to reach port, their gear worked by the living dead. These visions had a basis in fact. Occasionally, vessels came across drifting hulks whose crews had fallen victim to disease or starvation.

In Henry's day, ships bound for the New World did not sail directly across the Atlantic. Instead, they shaped a course to pick up the trade winds off the African coast, west of the Canary Islands. Produced by cool air flowing from the poles toward the equator, the trade winds were God's gift to mariners. Due to the

Finding a gigantic monster resting on the surface of the ocean, sailors mistook it for an island and made camp "ashore." The fire awoke the monster, which then attacked their ship. In this drawing from the early 1600s, the monster has pulled up the anchor and is about to crush the vessel and eat its crew.

Flying fish land on the deck of Francis Drake's *Golden Hind* during his voyage around the world in 1579–1580. Attacked by larger fish, the flying fish sought safety on the ship's deck, only to be eaten by the crew.

Earth's rotation, they blow from an easterly direction instead of from the north and south. Once a vessel found the "trades," the winds carried it across the ocean in almost a straight line.

Then things got easier, and everyone could relax at least a little. Sailors and passengers scanned the sea and sky, marveling at the Creator's handiwork. As the ship plowed ahead, porpoises swam alongside, and swarms of flying fish, chased by dolphins, leapt out of the water. Unable to "fly" very far, hundreds of them landed on the ship's deck, a tasty treat for all aboard.

Yet danger always lurked nearby. One vessel, for example, ran into a whale just as it was emerging from a deep dive. The impact smashed the ship's bow; it quickly sank with all aboard. Another

This plate from Edward Barlow's *Journal of His Life at Sea in King's Ships* is titled "The true picture of **A Shark the Most Ravenous Fish that Swims in the Sea.**" Sailors dreaded falling overboard, into the jaws of these ferocious creatures.

time, a giant swordfish thrust its six-foot sword through a ship's side, scaring the passengers and giving the sailors a good laugh.

Nobody laughed at sharks, though. You could stand on deck for hours, watching their triangle fins cutting back and forth across the wake. Always hungry, sharks followed ships to eat their garbage—not to mention anyone who happened to fall overboard. A Catholic priest told how a mariner "chanced to be a most unfortunate prey of one of them. Before any boat could be sent out to help him, he was seen to be pulled thrice under water by the monster, who devoured a leg, an arm, and part of his shoulder."[28] Sailors hated the big fish and took pleasure in killing them. Englishmen speared sharks with harpoons or caught them on hooks baited with meat. Spaniards lassoed them on strong lines, then shot them with muskets.

Henry must have admired the sailors' ability to entertain themselves. Between watches, they told stories and sang favorites like "The Stormy Winds Do Blow," "Neptune's Raging Fury," and "The Gallant Seaman's Suffering." Most vessels carried "musickers"—drummers, fifers, fiddlers, trumpeters—who amused their comrades with lively tunes. If they were really in the mood, sailors chose partners and danced jigs. Crews also acted in their own plays, "homely drolls and farces" with language to make a preacher blush.[29] Mostly they gambled with cards and dice. Jack Tar would bet on anything from how many porpoises would leap out of the water in a given period of time to the length of the largest rat that would be killed before sundown. Gambling addicts bet until they lost everything, including the clothes off their backs. The captain usually gave them a whipping for the good of their souls and a few rags to cover their nakedness.

And so the days turned into weeks. By the sixth week, the crew showed signs of restlessness. A transatlantic voyage, they knew, should take from forty-three to forty-six days, never less. For day number forty-seven to pass without a sign of land meant the ship had strayed off course, a dangerous error when food and water were running low.

Sailors could read the signs like an open book. When approaching the Caribbean, the sun glared with an intensity unknown in northern latitudes. At night the ship's bow cut a silvery streak in the water, and the tropical sky sparkled with countless stars. The water gradually changed from the deep blue of mid-ocean to turquoise and jade green, a sure sign of land. Land birds skimmed over the swells or perched on the rigging. Logs and branches with green leaves drifted past. On deck, an "old salt" drew up buckets of water and held them to his lips; the less salt he tasted, the closer they were to land. In the crows' nests, lookouts strained their eyes, eager for the silver coins that went to the lucky fellow who sighted land first.

One morning, a lookout saw a cloud formation on the horizon. No dark storm cloud, it hung white and fluffy in the gentle breeze. Before long everyone had gathered on the main deck, pointing toward the cloud with growing excitement. Hours passed. The ship moved ahead slowly, effortlessly, as if obeying a force beyond human comprehension.

Then it happened. An excited call came from aloft. "Land ho! Land ho!"

Two
The Making of
a Buccaneer

"A bolder race of men, both as to personal valor and conduct, certainly
never yet appeared on the liquid element or dry land."
—John Esquemeling, *The Buccaneers of America, 1674*

Mystery will always surround Henry Morgan's early
years in the West Indies. Although he probably landed on Barbados, England's most valuable island possession in 1654, there is
no record of his having lived there. Nor do we know how he
earned a living. Nevertheless, we can describe at least some of his
experiences with certainty, since they belonged to all newcomers
to the islands.

New arrivals had to become "seasoned"; that is, they had to
adapt physically to the tropics. This was the most difficult adjustment Europeans had to make. Accustomed to cooler weather
even in summer, settlers described the Caribbean climate as a suffocating combination of heat and humidity—"truly hellish, all torment and inconvenience," as one settler put it. The West Indian
sun is broiling hot, relieved only by "the Doctor," nightly sea
breezes. Day or night, however, the humidity feels like a wet

blanket held over your face. "The air there," a traveler wrote of Barbados, "is so moist, that if any instrument of steel is never so clean, let it lie one night exposed to the air, it will be rusty next morning."[1]

Newcomers found it difficult to sleep under such conditions. Before long, they discarded their feather beds in favor of the Indian's "string bed," or *hammacka*. The Abbé du Tertre, a French priest, praised this "blessed" aid to sleep. He described hammocks as "hanging cotton beds in which they [whites] sleep like savages; and besides that the custom is very convenient; it is not expensive because no pillows, sheets or quilts are necessary, so that a good cotton bed lasts a man for his life."[2]

Finding a comfortable bed, however, was only the first step in the seasoning process. Sleeping amid swarms of gnats was next to impossible. "True it is that in the daytime they are not very troublesome," a sufferer recalled. But at night these tiny terrors, almost invisible to the naked eye, "do bite so sharply upon the flesh as to create little ulcers therein. Whence it often comes that the face swells and is rendered hideous to the view."[3]

The climate combined with poor sanitation to spread disease. The worst diseases followed Europeans across the Atlantic. Rats, for example, carried the fleas that carried bubonic plague, or the "Black Death," which had wiped out a third of Europe's population during the Middle Ages. Bubonic plague did not exist in the West Indies until the first white settlers arrived. Once ashore, however, it spread like wildfire. From 1647 to 1649, plague borne by infected rats killed over six thousand settlers in Barbados alone. Similarly, mosquitoes spread yellow fever, a disease brought by slave ships from Africa. Dysentery, a severe form of diarrhea, filled colonial graveyards. So did human greed.

Planters worked indentured servants without pity, and few lived to the end of their contracts. Slaves received slightly better treatment, because they cost more and were lifetime investments. Since black people came from a tropical land, they adjusted more easily to the West Indian climate than Europeans did.

Somehow the young Welshman survived the seasoning process. Even if he worked on a plantation, it could not have been for very long. Within a year or two, Morgan decided upon a career and boarded a ship bound for the island called Tortuga.

Columbus discovered that island during his first voyage. Located just a few miles off the northwest coast of Hispaniola, it reminded him of an immense sea turtle resting on the water's surface, so he named it *La Tortuga*, the Turtle. Twenty-five miles in length, it was a natural fortress, accessible to ships only by a small harbor on the south side. Settled by fugitives from Hispaniola, it became the stronghold of a savage breed of men who called themselves "Brethren of the Coast." History knows them as the buccaneers.

It happened this way. Crews homeward bound from the English, French, and Dutch islands found Hispaniola's northern coast an ideal place to rest and make last-minute repairs before braving the stormy Atlantic. The Arawak Indians called this area Haiti, or the "High Country," land of the Thunder Gods. Haiti has a jagged coastline broken by countless creeks, inlets, and bays studded with coral reefs. Beyond the beaches lie freshwater streams, forested hillsides, and rolling savannas. Spaniards lived in and around the city of Santo Domingo to the southeast, but the High Country lay abandoned for generations. Most settlers had left when the soil lost its fertility as a result of overcultivation; others departed to join the conquistadores in their search for trea-

sure. Only tumbledown buildings and the descendants of abandoned farm animals—cattle, hogs, horses—remained behind. With plenty to eat and no natural enemies, the animals multiplied. Thus, by the early 1600s, Haiti had become a vast hunting ground with game free for the taking.

Landing parties shot game for their cooking pots. Unfortu-

A watercolor map of Tortuga painted about the year 1610.

nately, they could not take their kill on board, since meat spoils quickly in the tropics. Now and then, however, sailors deserted in small groups to live as hunters. During their wanderings, they met Arawak hunting parties. Remnants of a once-numerous people, the Arawak had been oppressed by the Spaniards since the days of Columbus. Expecting the worst, they fled into the forest the moment they saw these white strangers. But when they realized that these white men were not Spanish, the Arawak taught them to preserve meat in a special way.

The moment an Arawak killed an animal, he skinned it and sliced the most tender sections into long, narrow strips about an inch and a half in thickness. These he lay on a grill placed over a shallow pit, and then built a fire of green sticks. He called the grill a *barbacóa*, the origin of the English word *barbecue*. (Other Arawak words in common use in English are *canoe, hurricane, iguana, maize, tobacco, potato*.) The dampness of the wood prevented the fire from getting too hot and drying the meat too fast. Meanwhile, he added skin and bones to create a thick, tangy smoke that penetrated the meat. In the end, he had a tasty piece of meat that could keep for weeks. The Arawak called it *boucan*, or "dried meat." White hunters, mostly Frenchmen at first, called it *viande de boucanée* and themselves *boucaniers*—"buccaneers" in English.

Our chief source of information about the buccaneers is a man named John Esquemeling. Born in Holland in 1643, Esquemeling went to sea as a teenager, eventually reaching the High Country. A keen observer, he described his experiences in a book that first appeared in Dutch in 1678. He called it *The Buccaneers of America: A True Account of the Most Remarkable Assaults Committed of Late Years upon the Coasts of the West Indies by the Buc-*

caneers of Jamaica and Tortuga, Both English and French, Wherein are contained . . . the Unparalleled Exploits of Sir Henry Morgan. Despite its long-winded title, the book is at once a rousing adventure story and an invaluable eyewitness account. Not only was Esquemeling a buccaneer for twelve years, he met Morgan and joined several of his expeditions. Historians who have studied his book carefully agree that it checks with other records and is probably genuine. An instant success in 1678, it was translated into English, French, and Spanish. In the twentieth century, it has been reprinted several times.

Esquemeling describes how the fame of *boucan* spread from island to island. Captains began to make Haiti a regular stopping place on their return voyages. In return for simple trade goods—cloth, gunpowder, bullets, wine— the white hunters, the *boucaniers*, gave them hundred-pound bundles of *boucan*, enough to last most of the voyage. The buccaneers did such a brisk trade that markets sprang up along the coast at Port-de-Paix, Port Margot, and Cap-Français.

The buccaneers' numbers grew along with the demand for their product. We have already met their kind. Buccaneers were society's castoffs: jobless laborers, the homeless, runaway indentured servants, refugees from religious persecution, and men with nothing to lose but their lives. Among them were fellows with a capital *T*, for "Thief," burned into the palm of a hand or next to

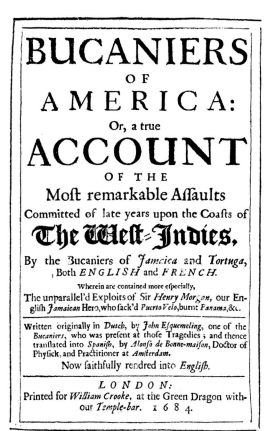

Title pages of the first edition of John Esquemeling's book *The Buccaneers of America.* Despite three centuries of historical research, it is still our best firsthand account of buccaneer life.

the nose. There were also Africans with raised scars on their backs and men of mixed race called *cimarróns*, from the Spanish word for "wild." *Cimarróns* were escaped slaves who had intermarried with Indians to form separate communities. These "black Indians" had scores to settle with their former masters. They made Spanish prisoners beg for the "mercy" of death before ending their torments.[4] The majority of buccaneers, however, were sailors fleeing the sea. Their attitude is captured in the words of this sailors' song:

> *O, the times are hard and the wages low,*
> *Leave her, John-ny, leave her.*
> *I'll pack my bag and go below;*
> *It's time for us to leave her.*[5]

The buccaneer lifestyle appealed to poor people. Yes, it was hard, but no harder than the lives they had always led. Few Europeans had ever known such freedom as the buccaneers enjoyed. Men of the High Country were their own masters, working only when they wished and only enough to suit themselves. No government of the rich made laws for "inferiors" like themselves to obey. No ship's captain could order them around. They had no watches to keep, no vile food to eat, and no rat-infested decks to sleep on. Best of all, there were no starters, no bilboes, and no cat-o'-nine-tails to make them cringe like dogs.

Buccaneers lived in groups of five to ten members, never more. Theirs was a man's world, with no room for girlfriends or wives. One might sleep with an Arawak or African woman for a night, but that was it. If he got serious about her, the group expelled him. Within the group, each man had a *matelot*, French

A maroon warrior, one of the runaway Spanish slaves who aided the buccaneers in the Caribbean and the Spanish Main.

slang for a special companion or comrade. Your *matelot* was at once your friend, family, and business partner. He stood by you through everything. In a fight, he covered your back, as you covered his. If you fell ill, he nursed you. If food ran low, you followed a simple rule: "Share and share alike." Between *matelots*, there were no locks, no doors, no sealed chests. Your *matelot* never asked for anything; he simply took what he needed from your pack without saying a word and without having to replace it. If you died, he inherited your belongings, and vice versa.

Becoming a buccaneer was almost like slipping off the face of the planet. Buccaneers were very private people. Most never spoke about themselves, and surely not to strangers or for any written record. Men with a "past," they guarded their identities like state secrets. Some substituted the names of their birthplaces for family names. Among the French, for example, we find Pierre le Picard, or Peter of Picardy. His comrades' names reflected certain personal qualities, like Tête-de-Mort, or Death's Head, whose face had been disfigured by disease. Others had nicknames like Chase-Afoot, Never-Fail, Hove-To, Pebble-Smasher, and Musket. Montbars the Exterminator prided himself on killing any Spaniard who fell into his hands.

A buccaneer usually wore a long mustache and a bushy beard that never felt the touch of a comb. To help stay cool, and to discourage lice, he kept his head shaved. His wardrobe consisted of a bandanna wrapped around his scalp, a peaked leather cap, and a long canvas shirt worn over canvas trousers held up by a rawhide belt. He made his own shoes "to size"; that is, he killed a cow and thrust his bare feet into the leg skins, which he cut off above the ankle and tied in place until they dried. The buccaneer never washed his clothes, so they became black and stiff with caked animal blood. For decoration, he might stick colorful feathers through his cap and march about with a parrot perched on his shoulder. Buccaneers, a traveler observed, loved "Parrokeets which talk English, Dutch, French, and Spanish, Whistle at command, small Parrokeets with red heads, very tame and pretty."[6]

Hunting parties left camp before daybreak. They went on

The complete buccaneer.
From the French edition
of John Esquemeling's
*The Buccaneers of
America.*

empty stomachs, refusing any food until each member of the
party had killed an animal. A pack of dogs ran ahead to flush out
the game. The Spaniards had originally used these dogs, called
mastiffs, to terrify the Arawaks, only to have them return to the
wild when they abandoned the High Country. Esquemeling saw
these ferocious dogs in action. "They run up and down the
woods and fields commonly in whole troops of fifty, three-score,

or more together, withal being so fierce that they ofttimes will assault an entire herd of wild boars, not ceasing to persecute them till they have at least overcome and torn in pieces two or three."[7] Buccaneers took puppies away from their mothers to raise in their camps.

Each hunter wore a sheath with three or four knives on his belt. In his hands he carried a musket called a "buccaneering-piece." Built by French gunsmiths for this select group of customers, the weapon was the envy of soldiers. This polished beauty was five feet long, weighed twenty pounds, and fired a one-ounce bullet. The buccaneer made his ammunition the way smokers once rolled their own cigarettes. Placing a piece of paper between two fingers, he set down a lead ball, covered it with gunpowder, and twisted the paper to form a *cartouche*, French for cartridge; the word means "rolled paper." He had to do everything just right. Fired with too little powder, the bullet would fall short; too much powder caused the gun barrel to explode in the hunter's face.

A buccaneer setting out on his morning's hunt with his musket, knives, and dog.

A difficult weapon to master, the buccaneering-piece required twenty-eight actions to load and fire. To load, the hunter took a cartridge from his bandolier, a belt draped across the chest having individual leather tubes. Biting off one end of the cartridge, he sprinkled "touch powder" into the pan above the trigger; a narrow channel beneath the pan led inside the barrel. He then poured the rest of the powder down the muzzle along with the lead ball, crumpled the paper into a wad, and pressed it down with a ramrod. To fire, he raised the piece to his shoulder and drew back the hammer, which held a smoldering cord or "match." Pulling the trigger forced the match into the pan, igniting the main charge and sending the bullet through the air. Experience made the men behind these guns the finest marksmen in the New World. Only fools would trade them shot for shot.[8]

The moment the dogs cornered their prey, a hunter dropped to one knee. Steadying his piece with a forked stick carried for the purpose, he aimed carefully.

Bang!

The musket's recoil knocked him backward. Recovering his balance, he ran to the fallen animal. If it was still alive, he reached for a knife and with a quick slash across the throat put it to rest. When everyone had made a kill, they built a fire and had a breakfast feast. Like the buffalo-hunting tribes of our Great Plains, buccaneers loved bone marrow. If they killed a bull or cow, they carved out the marrowbones, cracked them open, and sucked out the contents until their bellies swelled to near bursting. The hunt over, they returned to camp to cure the best cuts of meat, leaving the rest for the bugs and buzzards. Their diet never varied: meat and tropical fruits washed down with water. Flat stones became plates, and gourds served as cups.

As the sun set, each buccaneer lay down beside his *matelot* for the night. Lacking hammocks, let alone beds, they slept on bits of sailcloth spread on the bare ground. Before retiring, they prepared for the inevitable insect assault. Here, too, they learned from the Arawaks. Esquemeling reported that buccaneers "anoint their faces with hog's grease, thereby to defend themselves against the stings of these little animals. By night . . . they constantly for the same purpose burn the leaves of tobacco, without which smoke they were not able to rest."[9] They slept as close to the fire as possible, enveloped in smoke.

Spanish officials knew about the buccaneers but ignored

them because they seemed harmless. During the late 1620s, however, the officials changed their minds. With the Thirty Years' War raging in Europe and foreigners moving into the Lesser Antilles, these intruders seemed too close for comfort. Some day, Spaniards feared, their country's enemies might ally themselves with the buccaneers. By turning Hispaniola and the Lesser Antilles into naval bases, they could then attack the Spanish treasure fleets, crippling Spain's power in both the Old World and the New.

In 1629, a Spanish naval task force attacked a British/French colony on St. Kitts. After burning the plantations, troops herded the settlers aboard captured ships and sent them back to France and England. They sent them with a warning: If they valued their lives, they must never return to the West Indies. Nearly four hundred settlers managed to avoid capture by fleeing into the hills. When the troops left, they decided not to rebuild, at least not on St. Kitts. Traveling singly or in small groups, they made their way to other plantation islands and to northern Hispaniola.

The following year, 1630, Spaniards turned their attention to the buccaneers. Moving swiftly, cavalry units raided their camps in the High Country. Those not killed outright they tortured to death, or sent to a living death at hard labor.

Thus began the cycle of violence that would turn the Caribbean into a sea of troubles. Every buccaneer who lost a *matelot* took his loss personally—*very* personally. The survivors formed an association called the Confederacy of the Brethren of the Coast. Pledging themselves to eternal vengeance, the Brethren launched a guerrilla-style war. They struck when least expected, annihilating Spanish patrols and fleeing before rescuers could reach the scene. Soldiers retaliated by destroying the animals the buccaneers lived on, leaving their carcasses to rot in the sun. (Other soldiers would later follow their example. During its wars with the Plains Indians in the 1860s and 1870s, the U.S. Army encouraged settlers to exterminate the buffalo herds, the tribes' chief source of food.)

The Spaniards had started something they could not finish. Each attack sharpened buccaneer anger, further arousing the thirst for revenge. If Hispaniola became too dangerous, they fled to nearby Tortuga, where a village sprang up near the harbor. Whenever possible, they traveled back and forth between Tortuga and the High Country, always returning with fresh *boucan*.

Yet, times were changing. Not all buccaneers continued to hunt animals, or even Spaniards, ashore. Recalling their sailing days, they set out in tiny boats. Instead of pursuing the big treasure galleons, they prowled the coasts of Hispaniola and Cuba, pouncing on unarmed trading vessels. In reply, the Spaniards raided Tortuga. Any buccaneer caught off guard paid with his life. The majority, however, escaped easily enough. Groups of *matelots* hid in secret places or went back to hunting across the channel. When the Spaniards withdrew from Tortuga, they returned.

This game of hide-and-seek continued for a decade. Then, while Henry Morgan was still a child in Wales, a true pioneer in thievery stepped onto the stage. A person of intelligence and daring, we know him only by his first name, Pierre. Admiring comrades called him Pierre le Grand—Peter the Great.

Early in 1640, Pierre took twenty-eight men to Hispaniola in an open boat. Nothing! Try as they might, they found no Spanish prize worth chasing. With food running low, they knew they must return to Tortuga soon or starve.

At that point, Pierre had a stunning idea. He remembered that the humpbacked island commanded two key waterways: the Old Bahama Channel between Cuba and the Bahama Islands, and the Windward Passage between Cuba and Hispaniola. Treasure galleons had always used these waterways on their homeward voyages. Spanish seafarers thought them as safe as the waters off Seville. There was, however, one drawback. During the day, the trade winds blow in from the Atlantic, forcing sailing ships back into the Caribbean. From sundown to daybreak, the winds reverse direction, blowing toward the Atlantic. That was all Pierre needed to remember.

Toward dusk, he sighted a convoy in the Old Bahama Channel. The ships were making good headway under billowing sails decorated with scarlet crosses. A galleon had become separated from its companions and lagged behind by two or three miles. When lookouts reported a boat trailing them, the Spanish captain became indignant. "What then?" he snapped, his gentlemanly honor offended. "Must I be afraid of such a pitiful thing as that is?" Rather than show fear, he ordered the crew to maintain speed and stay on course. There would be plenty of time to overtake the convoy at daybreak, he believed.[10]

Meanwhile, Pierre vowed to capture the galleon or die trying. Slowly the buccaneers closed the distance. That big ship, how dangerous she seemed, looming up before them! To stiffen his crew's courage, Pierre drilled holes in the boat's bottom. He knew they would fight like demons, for survival now lay in victory alone.

Their boat was already sinking when it bumped up against the galleon's side. Esquemeling tells what happened next:

OPPOSITE: Pursuing the big prize. Artist Howard Pyle's portrayal of a small buccaneer craft pursuing a towering Spanish galleon.

Without any other arms than a pistol in one of their hands and a sword in the other, they immediately climbed up the sides of the ship, and ran together into the great cabin, where they found the Captain, with several of his companions, playing at cards. Here they set a pistol to his breast, commanding him to deliver up the ship unto their obedience. The Spaniards, seeing the [buccaneers] aboard their ship . . . cried out: "Jesus bless us! Are these devils, or what are they?" In the meanwhile, some of them took possession of the gunroom . . . killing as many of the ship's [crew] as made opposition. By which means the Spaniards presently were compelled to surrender.[11]

News of Pierre's exploit sped from island to island. It seemed so improbable as to be almost miraculous. Never had so rich a prize fallen so easily to so tiny a craft manned by such a small crew. Spaniards were dazed and astonished. Buccaneers were elated. Pierre had shown how to capture a large, heavily armed vessel at little cost. Although Pierre's comrades still kept the name buccaneer, no longer were they men of the High Country. In their rush to return to the sea, all but a few gave up making *boucan*. From now on, buccaneers would hunt Spanish ships full-time.

Tortuga became a magnet drawing adventurers from every corner of the Caribbean. Frenchmen for the most part, they welcomed all comers—all, that is, except Spaniards. Although Spaniards called them *corsarios luteranos*, "Lutheran pirates," they were neither. Many French buccaneers were Roman Catholics, as were their Portuguese shipmates. Unlike pirates, who attacked any vessel that crossed their path, the seagoing buccaneers preyed only on Spanish craft.

What a fantastic lot they were, this seagoing rabble. Thanks to Esquemeling's *Buccaneers of America*, we know about some of them. Among their ranks were fellows like Bartolomeo Portugués, or Bartolomeo the Portuguese, a short, dark man with long hair and a rat-tailed moustache. Said to have nine lives like a cat, his most spectacular feat came after his capture on a Cuban beach. Imprisoned aboard a galleon, he knew an executioner's rope awaited him when it reached port. He had no intention of waiting. During the night, his guard fell asleep over a wine bottle. Reaching through the bars of his cell, Bartolomeo slid the man's knife from his belt, stabbed him in the heart, and grabbed his keys as he fell forward. Yet he was still trapped. Although the galleon was only a few hundred feet from shore, Bartolomeo could not swim. Breaking into a storeroom, he found two earthenware wine jugs. These he emptied, recorked, and used as water wings! On shore, he met some buccaneers gathering firewood. Within a week, they captured the very same ship from which he had escaped.

François L'Olonnois hailed from the French town of Les Sables-d'Olonne, or the Sands of Olonne. Sent to the West Indies as an indentured servant, he underwent hardships that may have driven him insane. This cruelest of all buccaneers subjected captives to fiendish tortures. Even the sound of his name terrified Spaniards. After learning that he had put to sea, they fell to their knees to beg God's protection from *el diablo encarnado*, the "devil in the flesh." Justice came in a fitting way. One day, Spanish warships cornered him off the coast of Panama. After a sharp fight, L'Olonnois and his crew escaped, only to walk into an Indian ambush. Crew members fell in a hail of poisoned arrows. They were lucky; they died quickly. Their captain was not

BARTOLOMEW PORTUGUES

Portrait of Bartolomeo the Portuguese from Esquemeling's *The Buccaneers of America.* A fierce fighter, Bartolomeo captured many Spanish ships.

so lucky. He had also tortured Indians, and they repaid him in kind. Tribesmen, wrote Esquemeling, "took him prisoner and tore him to pieces alive, throwing his body limb by limb into the fire and his ashes into the air; to the intent no trace nor memory might remain of such an inhuman creature. Thus ends the history of the life and miserable death of that miserable wretch L'Ollonois."[12]

.   .   .

L'Ollonois the Cruel was probably insane. He is seen here cutting out a Spaniard's heart and offering it to one of his men to eat. The picture is from Esquemeling's *The Buccaneers of America*.

Henry Morgan joined men such as these at Tortuga. It was probably not a question of human attraction; for all we know, he despised their coarseness and brutality. He just accepted that business was business, and newcomers must start somewhere. Like his soldier-uncles, he had chosen an unforgiving occupation. Sea robbing offered no second chances, and your first mistake could easily be your last. Without the teaching and example of veteran buccaneers, the youngster would have no chance of success.

An anonymous seventeenth-century artist's impression of a West Indian hurricane. Each time these gigantic storms struck, they wrecked ships, destroyed plantations, and killed hundreds of people.

Crossing the Atlantic had given him a taste of seafaring. At Tortuga, Henry plunged into the subject. Most likely, he spent his "lost years" (1655 to 1665) at it. Buccaneering required a hands-on learning style, learning by hard experience.

Besides ship handling and navigation, Henry came to know the Caribbean as intimately as he knew his father's farmyard in Wales. The Caribbean is a fickle body of water. While the sea is beautiful and calm most of the time, within hours a hurricane forming off the western coast of Africa can lash it with winds of over 150 miles an hour. These winds are capable of uprooting trees and blowing houses away, even hurling cannons through brick walls. An aspiring buccaneer chief had to handle a vessel in winds that could shake her until her seams opened and she broke apart. To lessen the ship's resistance to the wind, and to keep her from capsizing, he must know when to chop down the masts, a dangerous maneuver but safer than losing them to the storm.

The young Morgan also learned that Native Americans were not all alike. The Arawaks, one of the most peaceful peoples on Earth, lacked even a word for war. Not the Caribs. Going stark naked, Carib men painted their bodies red and drew black circles around their eyes. Fearless fighters, they paddled their war canoes northward from jungle villages along the Orinoco River in Venezuela. Wherever they went, they butchered the Arawaks—literally, for food. Caribs were man-eaters; from their name, in its Spanish form, *caribe*, we get the words *cannibal* and *Caribbean*. During his second voyage, Columbus found Carib camps with "many men's heads hung up, and baskets full of human bones in the houses."[13] Caribs declared that Frenchmen tasted best, Englishmen pretty good, and Spaniards awful.

Henry became familiar with buccaneer ways. Upon deciding to launch a raid, a group of *matelots* would send messengers to spread the word among the Brethren. A few days later, volunteers would meet at a prearranged spot, each bringing his own weapons and ammunition. Buccaneers governed themselves by a set of rules called, in French, *la coutume de la côte*, or "the custom of the coast." These rules were nothing less than a democratic constitution, unwritten but known and respected by everyone. The Brethren had suffered too much under rules made by others ever to trust a leader with absolute power. Thus, in preparing for a raid, all participated in the decision-making. Similarly, while at sea the crew gathered "before the mast" to decide important matters.

At the first meeting, they would elect a captain by majority vote. Henry learned that buccaneer captains needed three qualities: courage, fighting skill, and luck. Purely military leaders, captains had absolute authority only while chasing and fighting the enemy. In everything else, however, they served at the crew's pleasure. A captain, therefore, could hold the crew's loyalty only by dominating it through his personality and filling its pockets with loot. A gift of gab—the ability to inspire others with words—also helped. The moment a crew lost confidence in its leader, he was out—or dead.

Henry found that buccaneers had advanced ideas about labor relations. Normally, European law permitted employers to do anything they pleased. They alone set business policy, fixed wages, and determined working conditions. If an employee got hurt on the job, too bad; he was on his own, even if that meant he and his family starved. The sea robber, however, was no ordinary worker. A partner rather than an employee, he had rights and obligations defined in a document drawn up before each cruise. Known simply as the "articles," the men endorsed it in a "round-robin" where each signed around the edge of a circle to signify their equality. Illiterates made their mark—an X or another design, such as a dagger dripping blood. Some pricked their thumb with a dagger and signed with the bloody fingerprint.

Articles covered all aspects of the cruise. In money matters, Henry learned, the first rule was "No prey, no pay." Buccaneer crews received no wages. As a partner, the individual's earnings depended upon the company's winnings. One successful cruise might bring as much reward as two years of backbreaking work in the merchant marine. If not, the buccaneer went away empty-handed.

The captain divided the entire "purchase," a polite term for loot, into equal portions called "shares." Each partner received something, although not the same amount. Shares were distributed according to skill. Captains received five shares; surgeons, gunners, and carpenters got two or three shares. So did the "sea artist," also known as the "wizard of the wheel." As the crew member most skilled in ship handling, he had to bring the ship into striking position without getting blown apart by enemy guns. Everyone else received one share, except cabin boys, who were entitled to only half a share.[14]

Articles also guaranteed a type of "workmen's compensation" insurance, a benefit unknown until the twentieth century. No partner could collect his share until the injured received their allowance. We see in the following table that different injuries had different values, expressed in pieces of eight or their equivalent in slaves. Depending on their sex, age, and working ability, a slave's value was expressed in both money and goods; that is, so many bales of tobacco, pounds of gunpowder, or barrels of beer per slave.

Since most people are right-handed, losing his sword hand made it impossible for a sea robber to "earn" his living. The loss of a leg paid less, since one could still fight on a wooden leg; "Peg leg" was a common nickname among the Brethren of the Coast. Buccaneers considered the loss of a finger or an eye a minor disability. A black patch over an eye was a badge of honor, proof of its wearer's courage.

Finally, articles enforced discipline aboard ship. Henry saw that his companions had few rules, but they enforced these strictly. Stealing from a shipmate, for example, concerned only the men involved. According to one set of articles, "If the robbery was only betwixt one another, [the thief's shipmates] contend themselves with slitting the ears and nose of him that was guilty,

Injury	Pesos/Slaves
Loss of a right arm	600/6
Loss of a left arm	500/5
Loss of a right leg	500/5
Loss of a left leg	400/4
Loss of an eye	100/1
Loss of a finger	100/1

and set him ashore, not in an uninhabited place, but somewhere, where he was sure to encounter hardships."[15] However, taking more than one's rightful share of the purchase harmed the entire company. This offense brought a sentence of "marooning"; that is, being stranded on a desert island with only a bottle of water, a pistol, and a single bullet. Days later, driven to madness by hunger and thirst, the culprit ended his misery with the pistol. Desertion and cowardice in battle also brought marooning. Buccaneers seldom used the cat-o'-nine-tails. They thought whipping too humiliating even for thieves.

Although generally peaceful among themselves, the Brethren did quarrel. Here, too, they went by the rules. Violence between crew members threatened unity and was therefore never tolerated. In such cases, the parties settled their dispute ashore according to the custom of the coast; in other words, with pistols, swords, and knives. When fighting with pistols, opponents stood back to back at a distance of ten paces, then turned to fire on a referee's signal. If both missed, they took up swords and knives. The first man to draw blood won. The loser had to abide by the verdict of blood, or die at the hands of his companions. In grudge fights, however, opponents tied their left arms together and went at it with daggers held in the free hand. Somebody always died. The historical record does not say whether Henry ever fought a duel.

Once buccaneers elected a captain and signed articles, their preparations for the cruise went into high gear. Food was never a problem for these able hunters. As a treat, they caught giant turtles, often a century old, which they lay on their backs belowdecks. These were mostly females, taken when they came ashore to lay their eggs in the warm sand. Turtles can live on their backs for weeks, and thus were a ready source of fresh meat. When it came to rations, everyone was equal. The captain had the same rations as the cabin boy, no more and no less.

Henry had to pitch in with the chores. Sailing vessels did not do well in the tropics. Seaweed fouled their bottoms, reducing speed and making it difficult to steer. Worse, the warm water rotted the caulking between their planks, allowing marine worms to eat into the wood. These tiny creatures are fantastic eating machines. Because one worm is able to lay a million eggs a year, they could turn a ship's bottom into a sieve after a few months.

Before going on a raid, a wise captain careened his vessel. At high tide, crewmen ran it onto the beach. Since a beached vessel is helpless against attackers, the men now worked feverishly. First they emptied the ship, then attached ropes to the tops of its masts. At the captain's signal, everyone gave a heave-ho, rolling it on its side to expose the bottom. Work details scraped off the sea-

Tortoises and sea turtles could be kept alive in a ship's hold for months, providing the crew with fresh meat.

weed, caulked or replaced rotten planks, and applied a protective coat of tar mixed with sulphur. After doing one side, they repeated the process on the other. Meanwhile, others "rummaged" belowdecks; that is, went through the holds to crush cockroaches and club rats.

For speed and ease of handling, nothing compared to the barque. Built of hard cedar wood, this sleek, low-lying craft measured fifty feet long by ten feet wide and had a single mast with three triangular sails. The barque handled like a dream, answering the sea artist's slightest touch on the helm. The much larger galleon, however, was a poor sailer, slow and clumsy even in gentle seas.

Maneuverability was vital, since barques seldom carried more than five light cannons, popguns compared to the armament of a galleon. A ship of between four hundred and seven hundred tons, the galleon carried up to sixty heavy cannons arranged in two or three tiers. Made of brass, these weapons fired several types of ammunition. Cast-iron cannonballs, or solid shot, weighed between twelve and thirty-two pounds apiece. A wooden sailing ship might take an awful pounding, but it could stay afloat if it didn't catch fire or explode. Nevertheless, solid shot could penetrate the thickest hull. The balls traveled slowly, punching jagged holes and sending wooden splinters flying about like razor blades. Chain shot—two iron balls attached to a chain—spun around with the force of a buzz saw to tear sails, cut ropes, and shatter sailors' bodies. For close-in work, gunners used canister shot, tin cans filled with musket balls and scrap iron. Like giant shotgun shells, the cans burst open, spraying a hailstorm of death.

A barque's guns might do well against small coastal craft and to repel boarders, but they were useless against a galleon. Conclusion: Avoid a gunnery duel by preventing the enemy from bringing his weapons to bear.

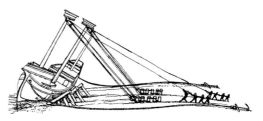

Experience taught Henry that twilight was the best time to attack. As the sun set, a small craft became barely visible in the vastness of the sea, while a big ship stood out against the horizon. In making his approach, the sea artist slipped into a galleon's wake and stayed there, exposed only to the four light cannons mounted in its stern. Every move the Spanish helmsman made, he copied instantly. As long as he kept astern, the enemy could not turn to fire his main batteries.

Careening a sailing ship was backbreaking, although necessary, work. Without periodic scraping of the hull, sea worms would have eaten their way entirely though the hull.

Sooner or later, Spanish lookouts gave the alarm. Shouting *"Luteranos! Piratas!"* they pointed toward the oncoming barque. Suddenly, as if someone had thrown an electrical switch, the lumbering vessel became a beehive of activity. Trumpets blared. Drums beat. Long battle streamers fluttered from the mastheads. *Arriba!* "Up and at them!"

The *slap, slap, slap* of bare feet on wood came from belowdecks as sailors rushed to their posts. While topmen hung nets from the shrouds to snare boarders, deckhands dragged "close quarters," heavy wooden barricades, into position. As an added precaution, they smeared the most vulnerable portions of the deck with lard and scattered broken bottles. Meanwhile, soldiers clad in steel breastplates and crescent helmets came topside. Armed with muskets and eight-foot spears called "boarding

Corvette

Brigantin.

Barque

Three types of buccaneer vessels. From the French edition of Esquemeling's *The Buccaneers of America.*

pikes," they formed ranks. Two-man teams mounted swivel guns on the deck railings; these were tiny cannons with turning devices for quick aiming and firing. Also known as "murdering pieces," they shot rusty nails and pieces of scrap iron.

Henry's excitement grew as the barque moved in for the kill. Aboard the galleon, the stern gunners went into action. *BAROOM-BOOM! BAROOM-BOOM!* The explosions sent the wheeled gun carriages rolling backward with lightning speed, crushing anyone unable to leap aside in time. Geysers erupted as cannonballs struck the water in near misses.

Henry's companions usually beat the Spaniards to the punch. During the approach, their best marksman stood in the bow with a musket. The barque bounced and lurched, but he never wavered. His eyes fixed on the galleon's gun ports, he waited for a target to appear. Whenever a gun port opened, he knew the men behind it were about to fire. In one swift movement, he raised the weapon to his shoulder, aimed, and fired. Instantly a shriek of pain came from the galleon. Without breaking his concentration, he reached over his shoulder for another musket, which a *matelot* placed in his hand. He fired often and true, until the gun port slammed shut.

Crouching to avoid stray shots, Henry and his companions waited anxiously. Now the sea artist really earned his shares. Swiftly closing the distance, he steered down the slope of a valley between two swells. Up ahead, the galleon climbed the other slope, towering over the barque like a floating castle. Ropes squeaked in their pulleys. Planks creaked. Cheers rose above the wailing wind. The barque kept coming.

Finally, the sea artist slid his craft under the galleon's overhanging stern. No mistaking it: this vessel belonged to Catholic Spain. Gazing upward, Henry saw a huge painting of the Virgin Mary holding the infant Jesus and the Spanish coat of arms, golden castles painted on a scarlet shield. Lanterns flickered behind a row of windows wrapped around the stern. The stern gunners dared not open their gun ports; even if they could, it was too late. The barque was so close that their guns could not be aimed downward at such a steep angle.

Safe for the moment, Henry saw the buccaneers go to work on the galleon's rudder. The Spaniards' hope of escape remained

A buccaneer gun crew prepares to fire. The man in front is about to set off the gunpowder charge in the touchhole at the rear of the weapon. The tub contains water, used to swab—rinse—the barrel after each shot. Unless swabbed with the device beside the tub, smoldering bits of gunpowder could set off the next charge, causing the weapon to explode and killing its crew.

alive only while their steering gear, a hinged device attached to the sternpost, was intact.

Yet that was not to be. As the marksman and his assistant stepped back, others took their places in the bow. Armed with wooden mallets and wedges rather than muskets, they grabbed hold of the rudder. While the first man held a wedge in place, his partner swung the mallet with all his might. *WHACK. WHACK. WHACK.* The wedge lodged between rudder and sternpost. *WHACK. WHACK. WHACK.* More wedges found their mark. That did it. Although her sails billowed, the galleon no longer answered to the helm. Her rudder jammed, she lay helpless in the water.

Their hearts pounding, Morgan and the others looked to their captain. He did not keep them waiting. Sword in hand, he raised his arm and pointed upward. "Away, boarders!" he roared.

At that very moment, sailors in the galleon's stern heard a whistling sound. Looking down, they saw buccaneers twirling silvery objects over their heads on ropes. Grapnels! Resembling barbed fish-hooks, only larger, grapnels were designed to grapple—grab—

Buccaneers boarding a Spanish galleon. The first man holds a flintlock pistol; his partner carries a boarding pike, a short spear designed for stabbing at close quarters.

something and hold it tight.

Grapnels flew upward, found the woodwork on the galleon's stern, and held fast. Instantly boarders grasped the ropes and, placing their feet against the vessel's side, began climbing like mountaineers. Higher, higher they climbed, until they reached the stern cabin windows. Pushing outward to gain momentum, they crashed through the glass panes feetfirst. As they landed, others scaled the galleon's side with poleaxes, large hatchets with a spike behind the head. By driving a row of poleaxes into the hull, boarders made an effective ladder.

Stripped to the waist, sweaty bodies black with gunpowder particles, the boarders appeared (to the Spaniards) like demons in human form. Although they had left their heavy muskets behind, they were walking arsenals. Many carried two or three pistols in leather holsters slung across their chests. Accurate up to thirty feet, such a pistol fired a lead ball with enough force to drop an ox in its tracks. Even when empty, it made a handy club or missile to throw at a foe's head.

A buccaneer's main weapons, however, were his blades. Poleaxes could just as easily crack skulls as make ladders. Knives caused hideous wounds. But for sheer killing power, the cutlass stood in a class by itself. It consisted of a heavy blade a yard long, slightly curved for slashing. When wielded by a strong arm, it could lop off an opponent's head in a single blow, or cleave him from shoulder to waist.

After fighting their way topside, boarders swarmed across the deck to meet the enemy hand to hand; Spaniards called it *mano a mano*.

Buccaneers were not gentlemen; they did not believe in giving enemies a "sporting" chance. A fair fight, to them, meant doing anything to win. Henry would not have been surprised to see a comrade butt a Spaniard in the stomach with his head, then follow through with a knife thrust. Other buccaneers leaned forward to bite off a Spaniard's nose, or squirt streams of tobacco juice into his eyes. The battle could become so disorganized that one might accidentally strike his

Stripped to the waist and barefooted, a buccaneer prepares to hurl a grapnel at a Spanish galleon.

matelot. At such times, gold earrings became lifesavers. The reflection of the rays of the setting sun on earrings allowed comrades to identify each other amid the swirl of action.

In their excitement, many buccaneers did not feel their wounds, not even when bare feet trampled on broken glass. The deck ran red with the blood of the dead and wounded.

Spanish discipline began to crack under the furious assault. There was no need to kill everyone to capture a vessel, only the officers who directed its defense. At first singly, then in groups, the defenders lay down their weapons and raised their hands in surrender. While buccaneers rounded them up and threw the dead overboard, a surgeon tended to the wounded.

The aftermath of a fight was always the same in human terms. Weapons in Henry's day were as deadly as any in the twentieth century. A cannonball struck with enough force to tear a man apart, turning his bones and teeth into "bullets" that were able to kill or maim those standing nearby. Similarly, a musket ball did not make a neat, clean hole. It shattered bones and tore muscles away from arms and legs.

There were no painkillers. The surgeon's assistants laid a patient on boards set between two barrels and made him "bite the bullet"; that is, they put a bullet between his teeth to prevent him from biting off his tongue during the operation. The surgeon used the same instruments, unwashed, on one patient after another. For serious leg or arm injuries, he knew just one remedy: cut it off. An amputation, advised one medical writer, must be done "boldly with a steady and quick hand."[16] A cut with a knife and three strokes with a saw usually did the job. The surgeon then seared the stump with a red-hot blade to stop the bleeding and applied a paste of shredded rabbit hair mixed with beaten egg whites. Bandages might be anything from scraps of cloth torn from shirts to bits of sailcloth. This explains why, in Henry's day, at least one out of five gunshot victims died of infection.

Buccaneers had a reputation for cruelty to prisoners. That reputation, however, was only partially deserved. A lot depended on their past dealings with Spaniards and their losses during the fight. If they had received good treatment, they looted the ship and allowed it to go its way. If they had bad experiences, or had suffered heavy losses, they showed no mercy. They tied batches of male prisoners together and fed them to the sharks. Women without relatives to buy their freedom might be raped and then sold into slavery.

Viewed against the background of world affairs, the actions of the buccaneers did not amount to very much. Although annoying, they were mere pinpricks even to Spain's weakened empire. Yet change was on the way. In 1655, an English fleet seized Jamaica. Neither the Caribbean, nor Henry Morgan, would ever be the same.

The Arawak called it Xaymaca, "Island of Wood and Water," because of the many rivers and streams that flow from forest-covered mountains to the fertile plains at sea level. Located ninety-five miles south of Cuba, this smallest of the Greater Antilles covers an area of 4,450 square miles. It is one hundred forty-six miles from east to west by fifty-one miles from north to south at its widest point.

Columbus reached Jamaica in May 1494, during his second voyage to the New World, and fell in love with the place at first sight. After returning to Spain, he described it to a friend as an earthly paradise. The friend, echoing his words, reported: "It is

Serratura.

Military medicine as practiced around the time of Henry Morgan's birth. The standard treatment for a bullet wound in the arm or leg was amputation. Since there were no painkilling drugs, this drawing is unrealistic because the patient is too calm. Most patients screamed with pain or fainted from the shock of amputation.

the fairest island that eyes have beheld; mountainous and the land seems to touch the sky; very large, bigger than Sicily . . . and all full of valleys and fields and plains. . . . Even on the edge of the sea as well as inland it is full of very big villages very near together. . . . The [natives] have more canoes than elsewhere in these parts, and the biggest that have yet been seen, all made each with a single tree-trunk. . . . They have their canoes carved and painted both bow and stern with ornaments so that their beauty is marvelous; one of these big ones that the Admiral measured was ninety-six feet in length and eight foot beam [wide]."[17]

Despite its beauty, Jamaica failed to attract many settlers. Those who did come brought the full range of European diseases, and few Arawaks remained by the year 1650. At this time, Oliver Cromwell, the Roundhead leader, became interested in the West Indies. Cromwell called himself "God's Englishman." For him, religion and patriotism were different sides of the same coin. As a fanatical Protestant, he believed God had commanded him to destroy that "seat of Satan," the Roman Catholic Church. As an English patriot, he vowed to make his country the greatest in the world. Hispaniola, he believed, held the key. Its capture would lay the cornerstone of an English Protestant empire, allowing him to break Spain's monopoly in the West Indies and seize the treasures of the Spanish Main.

Cromwell prepared for a surprise attack; that is, one without a declaration of war. To lead the soldiers, he named Robert Venables, an experienced Roundhead general. Command of the naval squadron went to admiral Sir William Penn, a man remembered less as a warrior than as the father of the founder of Pennsylvania, who condemned war as a sin against God. Before they sailed in December 1654, Cromwell proclaimed a crusade, or holy war in God's name. "Set up your banners in the name of Christ," he told his officers. "The Lord Himself hath controversy with your enemies. . . . In that respect we fight the Lord's battles."[18]

If they expected the Lord's help, they were soon disappointed. Within a month of landing near Santo Domingo (April 1655), a third of the soldiers lay dead, victims of tropical diseases. Their commanders knew that Cromwell regarded any setback as a personal insult. Rather than risk the executioner's rope for failing, they searched for an easier target. Jamaica fit the bill. The outnumbered Spanish defenders gave up or fled into the hills.

The conquest of Jamaica raised the stakes for both Spain and England. In a way, each became a prisoner of geography. For Spaniards, losing Jamaica was nearly as bad as losing Hispaniola itself. Lying across their shipping lanes and within striking distance of the Spanish Main, the island was a cannon pointed at their heads. For Englishmen, on the other hand, Jamaica became vital to the defense of their North American possessions. Virginia and Massachusetts Bay were already flourishing, while Rhode Island and Maryland were just beginning to prosper. Should Spain attack these colonies, English warships operating from Jamaica could strike them from behind. Yet the island proved easier to capture than to keep. Hemmed in by Mexico, the Greater Antilles, and the Spanish Main, Jamaica could be attacked from three directions at once.

Nature had blessed Jamaica. In addition to its strategic location, it possessed an enormous natural harbor on its southern coast. Protected by the Palisadoes, a nine-mile sandpit running parallel to the shore, this harbor is among the finest on Earth. Entire fleets can ride out hurricanes behind its shield of sand and coral.

At the tip of the Palisadoes, between the harbor's mouth and the sea, lay the fishing village of Cagua. There, in 1656, the English began work on a naval base. The work went slowly, too slowly for officers who had to answer to Cromwell. They needn't have worried. "Oliver" died soon after construction began, and in May 1660, King Charles II reclaimed his father's throne. The Cavaliers had won after all. England was a monarchy again. To

commemorate the event, the officers renamed Cagua. They called it Port Royal.

His Majesty had more important things
on his mind than Jamaica, however. Money
topped the list. With taxes higher than ever,
he recalled all naval units from the West Indies as a cost-cutting measure. Better yet,
having made peace with Spain one of his
first official acts, he did not need as many
warships as before.

Jamaicans disagreed. They understood, if King Charles did not, that peace
in Europe had never guaranteed peace
beyond the Line. Jamaicans knew that
Spaniards still hoped to retake the island.
Now, if they should strike without warning
(as Cromwell had done), English forces
could not reach Jamaica in time to do any
good. Given the distances involved, it
would take no less than six weeks to alert
London, another four to assemble a battle squadron, and another
six for it to arrive.

Early in 1664, His Majesty named Sir Thomas Modyford
governor of Jamaica. He could not have made a better choice. A
lawyer by profession, Sir Thomas had served as governor of Barbados before taking the new post. Experience had taught him not
to rely on Spanish goodwill alone. Spaniards might speak softly,
he explained, but talk was cheap. Deep down, they despised the
English. "The Spaniards," he wrote a royal adviser, "look on us as
intruders and trespassers . . . in the Indies . . . and were it in

Oliver Cromwell led
the rebellion against
King Charles I and sent
Admiral Sir William
Penn to capture Spanish
possessions in the
Caribbean. This is a copy
of a drawing based on a
painting by Robert
Walker in the National
Gallery, London.

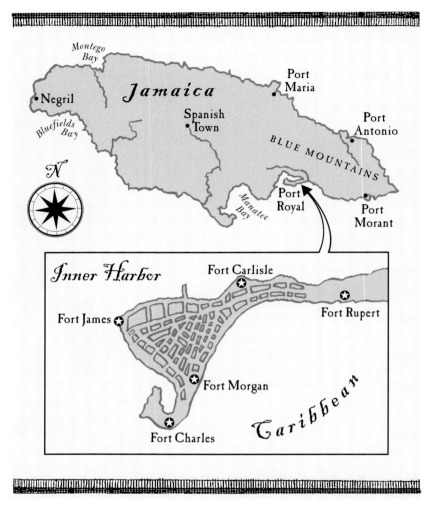

Map of the island of
Jamaica and the town
of Port Royal during
the time of Sir Henry
Morgan.

their power, as it is fixed in their wills, would turn us out of all our plantations. . . . Is it reasonable that we should quietly let them grow upon us until they are able to do it?"[19] The governor answered his own question with deeds, not words. Since he could not count on help from England, he decided to protect Jamaica in his own way. He invited the buccaneers to Port Royal.

The timing was perfect. Henry Morgan and his English com-

A portrait of King Charles II of England by Sir Peter Lely. King Charles knighted Henry Morgan and gave him high office in the government of Jamaica.

rades welcomed the invitation, especially since the French majority of buccaneers wanted Tortuga for itself. Moreover, they left not only because they needed another base, but because Sir Thomas offered them a chance to sail as privateers.

Privateers waged "private warfare." Although a treaty centuries later (in 1856) eventually outlawed privateering, governments had always issued "letters of marque and reprisal" to daring individuals. (*Marque* is an old French word for "going forth" or "crossing over.") Also known as "commissions," these letters were simply licenses to steal. With them, any citizen who could get a ship and raise a crew was free to prowl the seas and keep his winnings, minus a small share for the authorities.

In wartime, privateers were an inexpensive way to attack enemy trade, while allowing the navy to concentrate on the enemy's battle fleet. In peacetime, commissions enabled merchants to retake the value of goods stolen by foreigners. The merchant need not attack the guilty party; any of his countrymen, guilty or innocent, would do just as well.

Commissions separated "lawful" thieves from pirates. Since privateers sailed under a national flag, they could claim treatment as war prisoners if captured. Pirates had no country and flew the Jolly Roger. The word *roger* was English slang for a rogue or outlaw. Black in color, the Jolly Roger bore likenesses of skulls, crossbones, weapons, and hourglasses. These designs were not merely ornamental; they represented a certain attitude toward life and death. The hourglass stood for time running out and the shortness of life. The skull and crossbones represented the eternal sleep of death and the pirates' determination to kill or be killed. Henry Morgan, always a "lawful" thief, never sailed under the Jolly Roger.

Buccaneers acting as privateers became Jamaica's sole protection. Without these fierce warriors of the sea, the English authorities would have been ignorant of Spanish strength and intentions.

With their constant cruising, the buccaneers provided a steady flow of information. If the Spaniards were preparing a raid, the buccaneers struck first, throwing the enemy off balance until the danger passed. Always alert and ready to fight, the buccaneers supplied their own ships and weapons. Their services cost the government nothing.

Thanks to the buccaneers, plunder became Jamaica's chief industry. A Spanish spy wrote bitterly: "In general, there is no other way of making a fortune but by robbing Spaniards since, in Jamaica, it is impossible to make money."[20] Privateering would continue to flourish until white Jamaicans found other means to make lots of money.

Thames Street, Jamaica, lay just a few steps from the half-moon beach where returning buccaneers unloaded their prizes. Besides chests overflowing with pieces of eight and doubloons, they brought valuables of every description: gemstones, pearls, silks, spices, ornate mirrors, carved furniture, rare woods, and ambergris, a valuable substance used in making perfume. All except the coins were auctioned on the spot for a tiny fraction of their true value.

Port Royal grew along with privateering. In 1662, its permanent population numbered 670 white people and 1,500 full-time buccaneers who used it as their home port. Within eight years, the population rose to 2,000, with an equal number of buccaneers. The town also became a thriving slave market. Scarcely a week passed without buccaneers offering to sell "black ivory," slaves taken in raids on the Spaniards.

Port Royal was the first boomtown in the English-speaking world. Like California mining towns during the "gold rush" two centuries later, it was a wild and lawless place—a place where hu-

The passage of time and death as expressed in a trio of Jolly Rogers.

man life was cheap. Port Royal earned its reputation as the most evil spot on the planet. The town, an English traveler reported, was "as sickly as a Hospital, as Dangerous as the Plague, as Hot as Hell, and as Wicked as the Devil."[21]

Port Royal's trash-filled streets had one tavern for every ten inhabitants. No tavern ever closed its doors or went out of business for lack of customers. Buccaneers lived so dangerously, so close to death, that few gave any thought to the future. For them, only today mattered; tomorrow would take care of itself. Money, they said, "burnt holes" in their purses (pockets had not been invented yet). Flush with prize money, they headed for their favorite taverns, dives with names like the Blue Anchor and the Sign of the Mermaid. There they sat around rough wooden tables, gambling, carousing with "low women," and drinking.

Did they drink! They drank anything alcoholic: beer, ale, wine, brandy. Their all-time favorite, however, was Kill Devil or Rumbullion—rum for short. Made from molasses, Jamaican rum has always been potent stuff. Sir Thomas Modyford reported that "the Spaniards wondered much at the sickness of our people, until they knew the strength of their drinks, but then they wondered more that they were not all dead."[22]

Rum and riot went together. Buccaneers staggered through

the streets at all hours, shouting, singing, and cursing. Crazy-drunk and armed to the teeth, they did as they pleased, for there were no police. The sounds of their clanging blades and pistol shots sent ordinary citizens racing for cover. Exhausted at last, they slept it off on the beach, awakening with aching heads and empty purses. No matter. "A merry life and a short one" was their motto. There were always more rich prizes, weren't there? So why worry? Tomorrow would take care of itself.

Henry Morgan landed at Port Royal sometime in 1661. He stayed only long enough to sign the articles of the first outward-bound privateer he could find. His apprenticeship with the buccaneers of Tortuga made him a valuable addition to any crew. During this and later voyages, he earned a reputation for daring, courage, and calm in the face of danger—just the fellow you wanted on your side in a tight spot. Morgan also showed a keen business sense. Like all buccaneers, he liked his rum, perhaps too much for his own good. Unlike them, however, he never drank without first putting aside part of his prize money. Eventually, he pooled his savings with friends to buy a ship of their own. The crew elected him captain by a unanimous vote.

Captain Morgan seemed to have a magical touch, never making a serious mistake or pushing his luck too far. He also came to know all the "right" people. In 1664, the English king appointed Henry's uncle, Colonel Edward Morgan, deputy governor of Jamaica, in gratitude for his loyalty during the civil war. The grizzled old Cavalier introduced his nephew to Sir Thomas Modyford, who instantly recognized Henry's ability. Some day, the governor vowed, he and that young buccaneer would be allies.

Meanwhile, Morgan's ship joined two others in raids along

the coast of Central America. Starting at Mexico's Yucatán peninsula, they worked their way southward toward the Mosquito Coast of Nicaragua. The Indians welcomed them, as they had welcomed Francis Drake nearly a century before; they saw any enemy of Spain's as a friend of theirs. Although the buccaneers captured no treasure galleons, they sacked several towns, including Granada, capital of the province of Nicaragua. They returned to Port Royal toward the end of 1665.

Morgan learned that his uncle had died and found his cousin, Mary Elizabeth, in mourning. Drawn together by their loss, they fell in love and married early the following year. Like Henry's mother, Mary Elizabeth is a shadowy figure for historians. Apart from her name and the fact that she never gave birth to a child, we know almost nothing about her. We have no idea of how she looked, or what she thought of her groom's occupation. For his part, we know that Henry always referred to her as "my very well and entirely beloved wife."[23] After honeymooning on a plantation purchased with Spanish booty, he put to sea again. For the next five years, Henry would spend more time with his men than his bride.

This time he joined Edward Mansfeld, a sour-faced Dutchman who had already sacked St. Augustine in Florida and Old Providence Island in the Caribbean. Like Governor Modyford, he, too, quickly warmed to the younger man. They became good friends and close associates. Mansfeld made him second in command of his fleet of fifteen ships, with the title of vice admiral.

The Dutchman's death late in 1667 was a turning point in Morgan's life. Suddenly, everything came together for him. Gathering before the masts of their ships, the buccaneers chose him as their chief.

Sir Thomas Modyford thought it a wise choice. Early the next year, 1668, he signed a special commission. In it he authorized Morgan "to draw together the English privateers and take prisoners of the Spanish nation, whereby he might inform of the intention of that nation to invade Jamaica."[24] So, with the governor's blessing, Henry Morgan set out to make himself the terror of the Spanish Main. He was thirty-three years old.

Three
Admiral Morgan and His Old Privateers

"I assure your Honor that no man whatever knows better, can outdo or give so clear an account of the Spanish force, strength, or commerce...Admiral Morgan and his old privateers...know every creed, and the Spaniards' mode of fighting, and be a town never so well fortified, and the numbers never so unequal, if money or good plunder be in the case, they will either win it manfully or die courageously."
—Surgeon Richard Browne to the Board of Trade in London, October 1670

Sir Thomas Modyford signed Henry Morgan's commission just in time. The ink had scarcely dried on the paper when a buccaneer vessel arrived at Port Royal with alarming news. Only a few days earlier, she had captured a Spanish merchant ship off Hispaniola. Among the passengers was an army officer stationed in Havana, capital of the island of Cuba. After some hard-fisted "questioning" by the crew, the officer revealed plans for an attack against Jamaica. Was he telling the truth, or just saying what he thought his captors wished to hear? If he was right, how large a force would the Spaniards send? When would it sail? From where? The buccaneer chief must find the truth.

Morgan did not conceal his purpose. To recruit fighting men, he announced the expedition with a public display. Early in February 1668, a three-man team paraded through the streets of Port Royal. The flag bearer led the way, waving an English flag as proof of the expedition's legality. While the drummer beat a long roll to attract attention, the crier's voice rose above the street noises. A beefy fellow with apple red cheeks and a putty nose, he wore a scarlet coat and a white wig with ringlets down to his shoulders. The crier began with the traditional "Hear ye! Hear ye!" The rest was pure theater. Every able-bodied man, he announced, should join "Harry" Morgan's bold lads at the South Cays, a group of low-lying desert islands off the southern coast of Cuba. Brave hearts! Stout fighters! Do not miss the chance of a lifetime! Make the Spaniard howl! Fill your purse with his gold! It went without saying, of course, that they would observe the old rule of "no prey, no pay." Meanwhile, similar teams roused the French on Tortuga.

In less than a month, nearly seven hundred men assembled at a tiny cay. Although operating under Morgan's commission, they followed the custom of the coast. Like any buccaneer captain, Morgan could not do whatever he pleased. Whether it pleased him or not, he had to follow democratic rules. Before setting out, therefore, he observed all the requirements. After a formal article signing, his captains met to select a target for their crews' approval. The chief proposed a raid on Havana itself. Not only was Havana the largest city in the West Indies, the treasure galleons (as we shall see) visited its harbor regularly. Buccaneers might easily win a year's purchase at a single blow.

Yet it was not to be. No sooner did Morgan say the word "Havana," when the grumbling began. Oh, no! Not that awful place! Many knew the city only too well, having spent time in its jails and at forced labor on its docks and fortifications. As Spain's chief naval station in the New World, Havana was a natural fortress made even stronger by the best military engineers. Ships

approached the harbor through a narrow channel guarded by El Morro, a massive stone barricade bristling with cannons. Even if their flimsy craft slipped past the guns, doubters said, they simply did not have enough men to capture a city with a population of over fifteen thousand people.

Morgan knew how to seize an opportunity, turn it to advantage, and swing the buccaneers into line. He also knew when to back down—the sign of a shrewd leader. Rather than provoke a quarrel by insisting on Havana, he asked for suggestions. After further discussion, the captains voted for Puerto Príncipe, Cuba. Located twenty miles inland from the coast, this town of two thousand was a center of the island's flourishing tobacco trade. Their chief nodded in agreement. Let it be Puerto Príncipe!

On the night of March 28, 1668, twelve ships, none larger than seventy tons, glided into the Gulf of Anna Maria. Moving slowly, without lights, they found a small bay and anchored until sunrise. It would then be Ascension Day, a holy day commemorating Christ's ascension into Heaven. The buccaneers meant to celebrate the sacred event in their own fashion.

Morgan had a prisoner aboard his ship, a Spaniard whose name has been lost to history. Assuming that he did not understand English, the captains discussed the attack while he sat in the next cabin. Since the cabin wall was merely a thin wooden partition, the Spaniard heard every word they said. Not only did they name their target, they went over their plans in detail. That was a mistake, since the fellow apparently understood English.

Toward midnight, when things became as quiet as they ever did aboard a buccaneer vessel, a soft *splash* came from the starboard, or right, side of the vessel. Nobody heard the prisoner go over the side, or saw him swimming toward the beach. After an

OPPOSITE: An illustration of the harbor of Havana, Cuba, in the days of the buccaneers. The city was so well defended that Henry Morgan dared not attack.

all-night walk, he reached Puerto Príncipe and knocked at the door of the *alcalde*, or mayor. Landing parties were already rowing toward shore when the mayor sent a slave to the church of La Merced with an urgent message. Moments later, the priest clambered up a ladder into the steeple. After pausing to take a deep breath, he pulled the bell ropes with all his strength.

BONG! BONG! BONG! BONG! The metallic clanging echoed through Puerto Príncipe, rousing its citizens. They needed no questions or explanations. Spanish settlers had grown used to coastal raids, and people living inland constantly rehearsed their reactions in their minds, should the real thing come. Rubbing the sleep from their eyes, they leapt from their beds, ready for action. Families cooperated in throwing their valuables into wells, burying them in gardens, or hiding them in the woods.

Meanwhile, the town's defenders prepared for battle. Puerto Príncipe was laid out in typical Spanish style, with a central *plaza*, or square, where the main streets joined. Grabbing their weapons, eight hundred soldiers and civilian volunteers reported for duty in the *plaza*.

The mayor, who also happened to be the military commander, planned a forward defense. Rather than fight within the town, risking its destruction by fire, he posted his men across the road to intercept the invaders. To slow their advance and upset their marching formation, he ordered trees cut down and placed in their way. Then he waited.

Morgan showed that he was his uncles' nephew. His soldiering relatives had been in many tight spots during their careers but usually came out on top. Like them, Henry rose to the challenge. He had a quality common to all great fighters: self-control. The more dangerous a situation became, the calmer he grew and the more clearly he thought. Finding the road blocked, he led the column through some woods on the right. The detour was rough going, but it took them around the Spanish defenses, forcing the mayor to shift his men. Flustered by the unexpected change, they turned to face the enemy.

Emerging from the woods, the buccaneers prepared for battle. The English contingent probably included veterans of the European wars, who took their places with the ease of professional soldiers. At the center of their position a huge fellow squared his shoulders and held up a pole with an English flag. The flag, a red Saint George's cross on a white field, was the rallying point. Seeing the flag amid the confusion of battle would assure Morgan's fighters that all was well. Drummers stood in front of the flag bearer, ready to tap out their commander's orders. Amid the noise and disorder of battle, he could only send orders with drums and trumpets. Each drumroll and trumpet call signaled a certain action: advance, right turn, left turn, quarter turn, about face, charge, retreat.

The battle for Puerto Príncipe lasted four hours. Its mayor fell while leading a charge, and after suffering heavy losses his men retreated into the town. Weary but still game, they scattered in small groups to shoot at the invaders from windows and rooftops. That angered Morgan so much that he sent a messenger with this bloodcurdling threat: *"If you surrender not voluntarily, you shall soon see the town in flame, and your wives and children torn to pieces before your faces."*[1]

This sounds like terrorism pure and simple. So it is, by twentieth-century standards of warfare. Yet we must remember that Morgan was a man of his day, not ours. Modern rules of warfare define deliberate attacks on civilians as "war crimes" punish-

Henry Morgan wields a pike during the battle for Puerto Príncipe, Cuba. From the Spanish edition of Esquemeling's *The Buccaneers of America.*

able by death or imprisonment. In the seventeenth century, however, the law allowed a commander to kill everyone in a town if the defenders refused to surrender after receiving fair warning. Defenders who continued resisting when faced with certain defeat forced the attackers to lose men needlessly. Such behavior "justified" a massacre. The Spaniards knew the law, and they gave up.

Morgan herded the townspeople into the great church. Left without food and drink, they faced a man who would stop at nothing to get his way. Jeering guards warned that unless they paid up, "old Harry" would sell them in the slave market at Port Royal. With Morgan's permission, the prisoners chose four leading men to bring in all their hidden valuables. Meanwhile, the buccaneers took everything else worth taking: furniture, mirrors, drapery, carpets, bales of tobacco, barrels of sugar.

The four Spaniards returned a few days later with empty hands and plenty of excuses. Instead of admitting failure, they appealed to Morgan's greed. If he gave them another fifteen days, they promised to do better. He agreed.

Before they left, however, a patrol returned with a slave captured in the woods nearby. No common field hand, this black man wore clothes as fine as any gentleman's. He was a messenger carrying letters from the governor of the province. Addressed to Puerto Príncipe's leading citizens, the letters urged them to delay as long as possible; the governor was coming to the rescue with hundreds of soldiers. Then may God help those wretched sea robbers!

Realizing that he had wasted enough time, Morgan decided to make the best deal he could and leave without further ado. Guards dragged Puerto Príncipe's leaders before their chief. Without mentioning the governor's letters, he set his price for leaving: five hundred cattle and the Spaniards' help in butchering them. If they refused, he threatened to have his men torture them and their families into revealing where their valuables were hidden. Fortunately for the Spaniards, Morgan was bluffing—this time. Still, they could not afford to take the risk.

Early next morning, *vaqueros*, Spanish cowboys from nearby ranches, drove the cattle down to the beach. Urged on by Morgan, buccaneers and Spaniards went about their grisly task. Soon the beach became an open-air slaughterhouse, as they spread slabs of bloody meat on the sand and rubbed in salt to prevent spoiling.

Suddenly a quarrel broke out among the buccaneers themselves. A Frenchman was busily salting an ox when an Englishman stole the marrowbones. Since these were a delicacy, the Frenchman demanded "satisfaction" according to the custom of the coast. Everyone stopped working to watch the duel.

They were disappointed. Distracted by a friend's voice, the Frenchman turned around for an instant. In a flash, the Englishman whipped out a knife and plunged it into the Frenchman's back. Outraged at the murder, the victim's *matelots* drew together, their cutlasses and pistols at the ready. The English answered in kind.

Had it not been for Morgan, the two groups would have gone for each other's throats. Now he proved himself as much a diplomat as a warrior. Whatever his feelings might have been toward the French, he could not allow a brawl in enemy territory; besides, he would need the men of Tortuga for future expeditions. Stepping between the groups, he used the only weapon at his disposal: words. In the same breath as he ordered the murderer put in chains, he promised to bring him to justice the moment they reached Port Royal. He must have made a strong impression, because the angry men separated and returned to work.[2]

This drawing was done by an Inca Indian in Peru about the year 1600. Taken from an old manuscript, it shows a Spanish settler mistreating a native porter.

The fleet returned to the South Cays, where Morgan divided the booty. Yet his men were disappointed. Their loot totaled fifty thousand pieces of eight in cash and goods, not enough to settle even their tavern bills in Port Royal. Although Morgan kept silent, their grumbling probably delighted him. The buccaneers' need for money would whet their appetites for further raids, and soon.

Morgan had already selected the next target. During his stay in Puerto Príncipe, he learned that the Spaniards were, as expected, planning to attack Jamaica. Not only were they assembling a strike force at Havana, but also in towns along the Spanish Main. Already the governor of Panama had beaten the drums for volunteers. Arrangements were moving ahead slowly, which gave Morgan time to prepare. To throw them off balance, he meant to attack Puerto Bello, Panama, one of the most important places in the New World.

Two fleets of galleons sailed from Spain every year. Each fleet had a similar mission: to deliver colonial trade goods and bring back the treasure gathered during the previous twelve months. The first fleet, called the *Flota* (fleet), headed for Vera Cruz in the province of New Spain, otherwise known as Mexico. This bustling seaport received silver from mines hundreds of miles north of the capital, Mexico City. Still, as treasure went, Mexican silver was small change.

The second fleet, named the *Galeones* (galleons), set a course for the Spanish Main. Touching briefly at Cartagena in modern-day Colombia, it took aboard gold, emeralds, and rare woods brought from the interior. Continuing up the coast, the *Galeones* anchored at Puerto Bello to load the most fabulous treasure of all: the silver of Peru. In 1545, ninety years before Henry Morgan's birth, prospectors discovered a mountain of silver ore at Potosí. Dubbed by Spaniards "the King of Mountains, and the Envy of Kings," Potosí remains the richest silver deposit ever found on Earth.

For Indian slaves, going into the mine was a terrible ordeal. Overworked and underfed, few survived for more than a year. An anonymous Spanish visitor described how they spent their lives:

> working twelve hours a day, going four hundred and twenty and at times seven hundred feet down to where night is perpetual, for it is always necessary to work by candlelight, the air thick and ill-smelling being enclosed in the entrails of the earth, the going up and down most dangerous, for they come up loaded with their small sack of metal [ore] tied up to their backs, taking quite four to five hours, step by step, and if they make the slightest false step they may fall seven hundred feet; and when they arrive at the top out of breath, find as shelter a mineowner who scolds them because they did not come up quickly enough or because they did not bring enough load, and for the slightest reason makes them go down again.[3]

After melting the ore and pouring it into wedge-shaped molds, slaves loaded the finished product onto the backs of mules for the journey down the western slopes of the Andes Mountains. Arriving at the shore of the Pacific Ocean, they turned the precious cargo over to dockworkers, who put it aboard ships bound for the city of Panama sixteen hundred miles to the north. At Panama, the silver joined another treasure stream: gold from Central America and pearls from the offshore islands. *Recuas*, or mule trains, then carried everything over *El Camino de Oro*, the Gold

Road, a sixty-mile jungle trail to Puerto Bello on the Caribbean coast to await the arrival of the *Galeones*. When fully loaded, *Galeones* and *Flota* assembled at Havana for the voyage home.

Puerto Bello means "Beautiful Port." (Englishmen pronounced it "Portobello" or "Porto Bello.") Jungle-clad mountains surround the town, and it commands a spectacular view of the Caribbean. Yet nobody in the 1600s came to Puerto Bello for the scenery. The town existed for only two purposes: trade and treasure. Its normal population of two thousand swelled to three times that number when the *Galeones* arrived. A fair sprang up

Silver Mountain, Potosí, as seen by an anonymous Spanish artist about the year 1584.

Indian workers descend into the heart of Potosí, the richest silver mine on Earth.

along the waterfront, drawing merchants from every corner of the Spanish Main. One could wander for days among booths displaying all kinds of goods for sale. Some merchants auctioned naked slaves brought directly from Africa. Jugglers and acrobats performed hair-raising stunts for a few copper coins. Every night people crowded into tents for a fandango, a Spanish ball with gay music and wild dancing.

At such times, prices soared. Although he nearly went broke paying for his rented "mouse hole," Thomas Gage, an English Catholic priest, got his money's worth. Father Gage had the experience of a lifetime in Puerto Bello. The town overflowed with treasure. "What most I wondered [at]," he recalled, "was to see the *recuas* of mules which came thither from Panama, laden with wedges of silver. In one day I told [counted] two hundred mules laden with nothing else, which were unladen in the market-place, so that there the heaps of silver wedges lay like heaps of stones in the streets, without any fear or suspicion of being lost."[4]

Spaniards said that God made Puerto Bello's harbor, but Satan made its climate. The town received over one hundred inches of rain a year. Nowadays, air-conditioning and proper sanitation make life bearable there. In the seventeenth century, however, the sweltering climate, swarms of insects, and the odor of rotting vegetation made a deadly combination. Father Gage did not exaggerate when he called it the most dangerous place in the New World. "Especially when the fleet is there, it is an open grave ready to swallow a good part of the numerous people which at that time resort to it. That was seen the year that I was there [1637], when about five hundred of the soldiers, merchants, and mariners . . . lost their lives. They found it to be to them not *Puerto bello*, but *Puerto malo*"—the bad port. Nothing you did, short of leaving, offered protection against disease.[5]

Puerto Bello lay at the southern end of a harbor with high cliffs, each crowned by a stone castle on either side of the entrance. On the right side, separated from the town by a shallow river, stood Santiago de la Gloria, its main stronghold and military headquarters. On the left side, diagonally across the way, towered the castle of San Felipe, nicknamed *Todo Fierro*, "All Iron," because of its many iron cannons. Any ships caught in the crossfire of the castles' guns had little chance of surviving. They would be blown to bits within minutes.

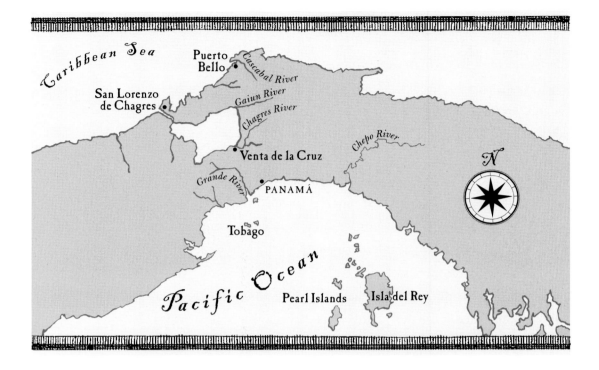

The Isthmus of Panama.

Equally dangerous, the castle of San Jerónimo stood on a small peninsula jutting into the harbor from the town itself. Not only did San Jerónimo's guns dominate the harbor, they commanded the road over which the mule trains traveled from the city of Panama. Puerto Bello's defenders never sent scouting parties into the jungle or patrolled the coast. Why bother? Their town was stronger than any invasion force. In 1596, while its defenses were still incomplete, Sir Francis Drake had failed to break through with a fleet of twenty-seven warships. England's greatest naval hero died of disease aboard his flagship outside the harbor.

Henry Morgan believed he could do better. Late in June 1668, he summoned the buccaneers again. After the usual article signing, he proposed a target. His listeners could scarcely believe their ears. Puerto Bello! Why choose that city? Next to Havana

and Cartagena, it was the strongest place in the New World. Attacking it was plain suicide. Suicide! If Harry wanted to kill himself, let him go alone, with their blessings. Only do not expect others to follow.

There were plenty of brave men among the buccaneers. Yet a man who combined intelligence, skill, and courage as Morgan did was rare. Rather than take no for an answer, he walked among the grumblers without showing any sign of fear. His eyes darted from face to face, but he said nothing. Men turned aside, unable to meet his gaze. Finally, in a firm voice, he appealed to both their pride and greed. *"If our number is small, our hearts are great. And the fewer persons we are, the more union and better shares we shall have in the spoil."*[6] That did it! The moment he finished, they roared their approval; all, that is, except the French. Rejecting such a risky scheme, they returned to Tortuga.

Morgan headed south with 480 men and twelve ships. While

Castillo de San Jerónimo, Puerto Bello, Panama, as it existed about the year 1900.

the crews settled into their routines, he kept to his cabin, deep in thought. He had plenty to think about. To attack from the sea with such a small force was clearly impossible. He did, however, enjoy one advantage. The Spaniards had no idea that he was coming. Very well. He would strike when they least expected: suddenly and in the dark.

During the second week of July, Morgan anchored in Boca del Toro, "Mouth of the Bull," an inlet 150 miles west of Puerto Bello. Somehow he got hold of twenty-three canoes of the type used by the Carib Indians in their long-distance raids. These were ideal for his purpose. Each canoe was forty feet long and equipped with a small sail and paddles. Built low, they were practically invisible against the tree-lined shore.

Morgan left skeleton crews aboard the ships with orders to stay put until he sent word to come to Puerto Bello. The canoes set out under a full moon. Hugging the coast to avoid detection by passing ships, the buccaneers paddled by night and rested ashore by day. An Englishman who had once been a prisoner in the town and knew every inch of the way served as their guide. A brooding fellow with hate-filled eyes, he seemed to have but one aim in life: to kill Spaniards.

It took four days to reach a spot ten miles from the target. Clambering over the sides of their canoes, Morgan's men dragged them through the surf, hiding them in the brush beyond the beach. Then, at three o'clock in the morning of July 11, 1668, they vanished as suddenly as they had appeared. Nobody saw them. Save for a few bored sentries, everyone in Puerto Bello slept soundly.

The invaders moved along winding jungle trails, fleeting shadows in the moonlight. They walked single file, silent except for the occasional snapping of a twig underfoot. Mosquitoes hummed around them, but they scarcely noticed, thanks to their hog-fat insect repellent. Sweat soaked their bandannas and shirts, trickling down their backs. Although each man traveled as lightly as possible, he carried at least thirty pounds of gear. Besides the usual musket, pistols, cutlass, and knives, he had a sack of "grenadoes," crude hand grenades made of iron tubes filled with gunpowder. Ignited by a fuse, a grenadoe exploded into dozens of sharp fragments.

Three hours later, the column halted at the edge of a clearing on the outskirts of Puerto Bello. Although still dark, the sky was already purpling in the east. Only yards away, a lone sentry stood at his post, unaware of the eyes peering at him through the high grass. Morgan placed his hand on a buccaneer's shoulder and leaned over, his lips close to the fellow's ear. He must take two others and capture that sentry if possible, Morgan whispered, but kill him if necessary—only do it quietly. The man nodded and slipped away with the grace of a jungle cat.

A hand clapped over the sentry's mouth and a knife pressed against his back warned him not to cry out. Hustled to the rear, he found the buccaneer chief sitting on the ground with his back against a tree. Morgan gave him an offer he dared not refuse. He wanted information. How many soldiers are on duty tonight? Do they expect trouble? Is anything unusual going on in the town? After each answer, he warned the Spaniard to answer truthfully. If he lied, Morgan promised to have him killed in a way that would make him curse his mother for bringing him into the world. Shaking with fear, the poor fellow told everything he knew.

The buccaneers advanced toward the sleeping town, their prisoner leading the way. Moving down the main road, they passed through deserted streets and hid in the bushes near San Jerónimo. Atop the walls, silhouetted against the sky, they saw guards making their rounds. Some carried muskets, others halberds—heavy ax blades mounted at the end of eight-foot poles. So far so good.

Feeling their way in the dark, they loaded their weapons and lit their rope "matches," taking care to shield the glow with cupped hands. After a few minutes, Morgan ordered his prisoner to step out and deliver a message: Surrender at once, "otherwise they should be all cut to pieces."[7]

San Jerónimo's garrison consisted of regular troops and criminals forced to serve their sentences in the army. The equal of any buccaneer, these desperadoes received no pay other than what they scavenged from the dead, the enemy's and their own, after a battle. They did not scare easily. The moment they heard Morgan's ultimatum, they answered with their muskets.

A mob of howling buccaneers broke from cover at a run. When they reached the castle wall, some heaved grapnels while others threw grenadoes at the heavy wooden door, blowing it off its hinges. Within twenty minutes, fifty-six Spaniards lay dead and another seventy-four, dazed and bleeding, raised their hands above their heads. Little did they know that they, too, were as good as dead.

Morgan's men learned they were not the only foreigners in San Jerónimo. After overpowering the defenders, they explored the dungeons below the castle, a dark, dank place with green slime oozing down the walls. Following a row of dimly burning lanterns, they found eleven Englishmen, who identified themselves as the survivors of a thirty-man crew captured two years earlier. Now little more than bags of flesh and bone, the naked prisoners were chained to the walls of a dungeon twelve feet by ten feet. The tiny room reeked of urine and excrement, sweat and vomit. Until his escape from a work detail, Morgan's guide had been held in that very dungeon.

A rescuer recorded the prisoners' story:

> They were forced to work . . . from five in the morning till seven at night, and at such a rate that the Spaniards confessed they made one of them do more work than any three Negroes, yet when weak from want of victuals and sleep they were knocked down and beaten with cudgels. . . . Having no clothes, their backs were blistered by the sun, their heads scorched, their necks, shoulders, and hands raw with carrying stones and mortar . . . and their legs bruised and battered with the irons.[8]

The sight of these men threw the buccaneers into a frenzy. "Vengeance!" they shouted, waving their cutlasses. "Kill the Spaniards!" Without hesitating, Morgan ordered his prisoners, about fifty-five men, locked in a room above the fort's magazine, where the gunpowder was stored. After ordering his own men to safety, he had the gunpowder set off with a ten-minute fuse. An earthshaking explosion rattled windows in Puerto Bello, followed by an enormous fireball. Vengeance, however, was not Morgan's only motive. John Esquemeling, who was there, says he wished "to strike terror into the rest of the city."[9] Then, as now, terror can disorient its victims, spreading panic and paralyzing their will to resist.

As a pillar of smoke and dust climbed skyward, the buccaneers swept into Puerto Bello. They came like a human tornado, savage and irresistible. Separating into small groups, they raced through the streets, shouting, shooting, and cutting down anyone who stood in their way. Meanwhile, their chief sent five-man squads to search the larger houses and seize the Royal Treasury, a stone building used for storing treasure.

Townspeople, startled awake by the uproar, poured into the streets dressed in their nightclothes. Some wealthy citizens hid their money and jewels as best they could. Yet few were so clear-headed. Most simply ran about shrieking hysterically, not knowing what to do or where to go.

The *alcalde* was Don José Sánchez Ximénez, a tall, dignified man noted for his courage. Don José tried to halt the panic. He saddled his horse and rode into the streets, waving a sword and calling for people to resist the invaders. It was like pleading with a stone wall. Finally, he galloped home to his wife and daughter. Somehow he managed to lead them to safety in Santiago de la Gloria and then took command in person.

Don José knew what he had to do. His king had entrusted him with the defense of Puerto Bello, a sacred task in his eyes. Honor demanded that he do his duty at any cost, even his own life. Yet that was the easy part.

Duty clashed with humanity. Looking down from the castle wall, Don José saw civilians fleeing toward the gate, a mob of whooping, cutlass-waving buccaneers at their heels. Could he— *dare* he—harm these innocent fugitives? He faced an awful dilemma. By shutting the gate, many would die, and it would be his fault. Yet by leaving the gate open, even for a few minutes, the buccaneers would follow them into the castle.

Duty prevailed. Not only did Don José shut the gate, he ordered the gunners to fire into the town itself. Cannonballs

OPPOSITE: Buccaneers pursue the Spanish defenders through the streets of Puerto Bello, Panama. From the Dutch edition of Esquemeling's *The Buccaneers of America.*

whizzed overhead, smashing buildings and bouncing along the crowded streets. Civilians and buccaneers lay huddled together in death.

Morgan ordered his men to take cover behind rocks and bushes. To them, a besieged castle was merely a stone galleon stranded on dry land. Whenever a gunner showed himself, a sharpshooter sent a bullet in his direction. Gunners fell, but others instantly took their places. The sniping continued all morning, the Spaniards returning bullet for bullet.

Noontime. The sun hung directly overhead, glaring down on the crouching men; a buccaneer said it "broiled the brains." From time to time, to relieve the nervous strain, Morgan sent his men forward with grapnels and grenadoes. The defenders, however, stood firm. Urged on by Don José, they met the attackers with red-hot stones, boiling water, and "fireballs," earthenware pots filled with gunpowder and sulphur. Like modern napalm, a form of jellied gasoline, fireballs turned their victims into human torches. Screaming buccaneers rolled on the ground to smother the flames. Those who succeeded carried ugly scars for the rest of their lives. Those who failed died in agony.

A trumpet sounded after the latest assault. Slowly, cautiously, three buccaneers stepped from cover and came toward the wall under a white flag of truce. They carried a message from their chief. If Don José did not surrender at once, Morgan promised to give la Gloria's defenders a nasty surprise.

The mayor brushed the warning aside. Let *los perros Ingleses*, "the English dogs," go to the devil! He, Don José Sánchez Ximénez, would do his duty as a Spanish soldier should.

Morgan ordered his carpenters to make twelve ladders, each wide enough for four men to climb side by side. Ladders, of course, were the usual way of getting over the walls of a fortress. The problem, as always, was to cross the open ground between the attackers' starting point and the wall itself. Men carrying forty-foot ladders would move slowly, making excellent targets. And Don José's soldiers had already earned the buccaneers' respect.

The "surprise" Morgan had promised was brutal even by the standards of a brutal age. He had eighty priests and nuns dragged from their churches and brought to the front line. If they wished to live, he growled, let them pick up the ladders and march straight toward Don José's guns.

Stunned by the demand, they begged for mercy. Yet nothing could persuade Morgan to change his mind. Ignoring their pleas, he told them to pick up the ladders and get going—or else.

They obeyed. Stooping under their heavy burdens, the clergy marched toward the castle wall. Scores of buccaneers followed, bent low behind their human shields. Surely, their chief thought, no devout Catholic would strike at the clergy.

Morgan had misjudged his opponent. As the wretched mob inched forward, Don José ordered his soldiers to prepare to fire. Gunners trained their cannons on the open ground. Musketeers leaned forward, their weapons loaded and ready.

Shrill cries reached the mayor's ears. "The religious men and women ceased not to cry unto him and beg of him by all the Saints of Heaven he would deliver the castle, and spare both his and their own lives," Esquemeling recalled.[10] Although some tried to turn back, buccaneers pricked them forward with the points of their cutlasses.

"Nombre de Dios," "In God's name," a Spanish officer gasped. Those English devils meant to storm the castle over the bodies of innocents!

The soldiers watched helplessly. What should they do? Could they shoot down their own people to get at the demons behind them? If so, how could they live with their consciences? Would God cast them into hell for killing His servants?

Nearer, nearer, the crowd came. At first, it was merely a mass of vague figures. Then, suddenly, it dissolved into individual faces. Now the issue became personal. To the soldiers, it felt as if they were aiming at their loved ones. A musketeer recognized the nun who had tended to his friend's sick child. A fellow with a firepot saw the priest who had given him a blessing.

Don José took a deep breath. *"Fuego,"* he shouted at the top of his voice. "Fire!"

No shouts. No gunshots. Nothing.

His soldiers stood still as statues, unable to obey the dreadful command.

The mayor was not a patient man. He must stop those "pirates" before they reached the wall. Raising his sword for all to see, he brought it down with a swift, hacking motion. No one could mistake his message: This was their last chance. Don José would personally kill anyone who disobeyed.

Soldiers crossed themselves and whispered pleas for forgiveness. Then they blazed away with all the weapons they possessed.

A hailstorm of hot lead tore through the human shields. Agonized shrieks rose above the roar of the guns. Although many clergy fell dead or wounded, the buccaneers drove the survivors over the shattered bodies of their friends.

Finally, the ladders were placed against the wall and the innocents got out of the way. Up went the buccaneers. Whooping like wild men, they hacked away with their cutlasses. Soldiers fell with bellies split open and throats spurting blood. Streams of blood

Henry Morgan directs the assault on the castle at Puerto Bello, Panama. From the Dutch edition of Esquemeling's *The Buccaneers of America*.

flowed in the cracks between cobblestones, collecting in puddles. Morgan's men seemed possessed by the devil.

Spanish resistance collapsed under the fury of the assault. Only Don José stood firm. Buccaneers cornered him at the base of a tower, but he put his back against the wall, cutting down one after another with his sword. Although the mayor had no chance of escape, he defied them to do their worst. Suddenly, his wife and daughter ran from a building and fell to their knees before him. With tears rolling down their cheeks, they begged him to surrender if only out of love for them. He refused.

The buccaneers would have shot Don José on the spot, had their chief allowed it. Harsh as he was, Morgan still admired courage. And this Spaniard was the bravest man he had ever seen. Stepping forward, Morgan asked him to surrender; this was the only time we know of that he ever showed generosity toward an enemy. The mayor had fought honorably, he said, and nobody would call him a coward.

The courageous Spaniard could not find it within himself to give up. "By no means," he cried. "I had rather die as a valiant soldier than be hanged as a coward."[11] There was nothing else anyone could say. Morgan stepped back and nodded in the mayor's direction. A dozen pistol shots rang out. Don José crumpled to the ground and lay still, amid a widening pool of blood.

Next day, Morgan's fleet anchored outside the harbor, making sure to stay clear of San Felipe on the eastern shore. The castle's commander, however, was no Don José Sánchez Ximénez. Although he held a strong position, the town's capture had shaken his confidence. After a brief show of resistance, he surrendered on condition that Morgan spare the garrison. The buccaneer chief kept his word. The commander, however, was crushed. Ashamed at his actions in a moment of weakness, he took poison that same night. Castle San Felipe survived for another two centuries. In the early 1900s, U.S. Army engineers dynamited it and used the rubble to build the locks of the Panama Canal.

The buccaneers turned to their main business. Finding the Royal Treasure House nearly empty, they tortured men and women in order to learn where they had hidden their valuables.

Torture was acceptable according to the ethics of the seventeenth century; governments used it regularly. Buccaneers were men of their time, no better and no worse. As youngsters, most, no doubt, had attended public executions. As seamen, few escaped the whip or similar abuses. So when dealing with the hated Spaniards, they did what came "naturally." Although we can understand why they acted as they did, the fact remains that they often harmed people who had never wronged them.

Nobody ever accused Morgan of torturing anyone with his own hands. No matter. In his lust for money, he gave others a free hand. Spanish officials later interviewed the survivors of Puerto Bello. Their testimony, preserved in official reports, is enough to make one's flesh crawl.

The story of Doña Augustina de Rojos, the wealthiest woman in Puerto Bello, shows how cruel buccaneers could be toward women. Asked where she had hidden her jewels, Doña Augustina said she had forgotten. Morgan's torturers helped her remember. They tore off her clothes and put her into an empty barrel, which they filled with gunpowder. Then one fellow tied a smoldering rag to the end of a pike, held it under her nose, and repeated the question. She told him everything.

Doña Augustina was "lucky." Though terribly frightened, she had not been physically hurt. Many of her neighbors went to the rack, a device for slowly pulling a victim's arms and legs out of their sockets. Morgan's ships, however, carried no racks. Instead, his torturers "borrowed" the ones Spaniards used to force confessions from their own people.

A buccaneer named John Sayle described other, equally excruciating, tortures: "It is a common thing among the privateers, besides burning with matches and such-like torments, to cut a man to pieces, first some flesh, then a hand, an arm, a leg, sometimes tying a cord about his head and with a stick twisting it till the eyes shoot out, which is called 'woolding.' "[12]

Meanwhile, eight Spaniards escaped to the city of Panama. Augustín de Bracamonte, the provincial governor, set out at once with a rescue party as large as Morgan's entire force. The buccaneer chief, however, had taken the precaution of sending patrols into the jungle outside Puerto Bello. Warned of the rescuers' approach, he posted one hundred men along a narrow pass through which the trail wound. Dozens of Spaniards fell when the buccaneers sprung their ambush. Unable to break through to the town, they camped in the jungle, amid poisonous snakes and swarms of insects.

Next morning, a Spanish soldier approached Puerto Bello with a white flag of truce. Challenged by a guard, he handed over a letter from his master. Don Augustín came straight to the point: Morgan must leave Puerto Bello by sundown. If he refused this "generous" offer, the Spaniards would surely take no prisoners when they liberated the town. So, let Morgan choose between escape and death.

A sly smile crept over the buccaneer's face. It amused him that a Spaniard should demand anything after the ambush. Nevertheless, there was nothing amusing in his reply. Written in Spanish and signed "Henrrique Morgan," it came straight to the point. His Excellency must pay ransom; 350,000 pieces of eight, to be exact. If he refused, Morgan would surely burn Puerto Bello to the ground and show its citizens "the same kindness that the English prisoners have received in this place."[13] The Spanish authorities had tortured and killed Englishmen without mercy. So, let Don Augustín take heed, because turnabout is fair play.

The governor showed no sympathy for Puerto Bello. Its citizens, he replied, must pay their own ransom; there were other, better uses for the king's money. He closed his letter of response in an unusual way. After congratulating Morgan on taking such a well-defended place, he asked a favor. Could the buccaneer chief send him, please, a sample of the weapons his men had used in the battle?

Morgan answered as one "gentleman" to another. Of course he would honor the request. He sent a pistol and a handful of lead balls, not as gifts, but as a loan. His Excellency could keep them for a year, after which time Morgan would come to "Penamaw" and take them back.[14]

Don Augustín returned the pistol along with a flowery letter. In it he thanked Morgan for his courtesy, but said the weapon was nothing special; Spanish firearms were just as good. The pistol came with a valuable gold ring and a warning "not to give himself the labor of coming to Panama." If Morgan came to the city, he would not do as well there as he had at Puerto Bello.[15]

Morgan had the last word. Since the governor refused to pay ransom, he turned to his prisoners. Eager to get rid of their unwelcome guests, they offered 100,000 pieces of eight. Morgan accepted readily. He had lost only eighteen men in the fighting, but twice that number were falling ill each day. Rather than push his luck, he decided to take what he could get and depart. Within three days, the merchants of Panama lent their associates the full amount. The cash ransom and looted valuables made a hefty sum. Each buccaneer received a little over £150; that is, six times an average English town worker's yearly income.

Port Royal had never seen such a homecoming. Morgan's buccaneers, their purses bulging with Spanish coins, went on a spree.

They gambled. They womanized. They drank. Rum flowed like water, as did brandy and wine. One bleary-eyed fellow bought a seventy-gallon barrel of French wine. He rolled the barrel into Thames Street, stood it on end, and bashed in the top with an ax. Waving a pistol, he shouted rather than sang bawdy songs, demanding between verses that passersby toast his health— or else. Tiring of that, he cupped his hands and flung the red liquid at women, shaking with laughter as it splattered their dresses.

A buccaneer, armed to the teeth, poses before a large barrel of wine.

As with all drunken sprees, this one ended in head-pounding discomfort. Once the buccaneers' money ran out, tavern keepers refused to give credit, forcing many to go begging from door to door for food. Things became so desperate that they demanded their chief put to sea without delay, "for they were reduced to a starving condition."[16] He gladly obliged. Little did he know that he was about to escape death by a hairsbreadth.

In October 1668, the town crier announced that Morgan was assembling a force at Cow Island, a favorite careening spot off Hispaniola's southern coast. Eight hundred men and ten ships answered his call. Among them was a new arrival to the West Indies, the *Oxford*, a warship on loan from the Royal Navy. This sleek, three-hundred-ton beauty mounted thirty-six heavy guns and had come from England at Sir Thomas Modyford's urgent request. Assigned to patrol duty, her captain had orders to put his vessel at the governor's disposal. Modyford promptly sent her to Morgan to use as his flagship. In effect, he'd made Morgan head of the Jamaican "navy."

A few days after *Oxford*'s arrival, a French privateer out of Tortuga anchored nearby. A powerful warship in her own right, *Le Cerf Volant—The Kite*—also mounted thirty-six guns. Joined with the *Oxford*, they could have challenged any galleon to a duel. The French, however, had recently demanded supplies from an English ship, paying with a worthless IOU, which is short for I owe you, a term coined about the year 1618. Morgan's bullyboys demanded "justice," so he invited the French captain and most of his crew to a get-together aboard the *Oxford*. Rum flowed freely. When his guests got roaring drunk, Morgan locked them below-decks and seized their ship. He renamed it *Satisfaction*, no doubt a reflection of his current mood.

On January 2, 1669, the day after New Year's, Morgan called his captains to a war council aboard the *Oxford*. Everyone was in high spirits. After their exploits at Puerto Bello, they felt invincible. Nothing, they believed, could stop them. All they had to do was select a target and it would fall into their hands like ripe fruit off a tree.

They sat around a table in the ship's great cabin, discussing their next move. Captains mentioned several Spanish towns, but in the end they voted to attack Cartagena, the richest and most strongly defended city of the Spanish Main. Having made their decision, they feasted on roast pig and downed tankards of fiery Jamaican rum. When a fiddler struck up a tune, they wiped their greasy fingers on their shirts and danced a jig. Not to be outdone, *Oxford*'s crew also got drunk and fired the cannons just for fun. Night fell swiftly, as it does in the tropics. The salvos continued, echoing across the still waters of the bay, tongues of orange flame piercing the darkness. Then it happened.

Sailors aboard nearby ships saw a blinding flash followed by a clap of thunder as *Oxford*'s gunpowder magazine exploded. *KA-BOOM!*

Instantly the air filled with wooden timbers, metal fragments, and human body parts. Men shot upward, engulfed in fire, as if spewed from the mouth of a volcano.

Rescuers set out in longboats, but wherever they turned, they found only wreckage and death. Three hundred fifty English sailors either died in the explosion or drowned soon afterward. Of the French prisoners, confined directly above the magazine, not a piece of flesh or stitch of clothing survived. Yet the Morgan luck held firm—was, if anything, contagious. The explosion flung him and those seated to his right and left through the cabin windows, dropping them into the sea without a scratch. Those seated across from him vanished without a trace. At daybreak, an eyewitness recalled, looters rowed among the corpses "to obtain the spoil of their clothes and other attire. And, if any had golden rings on their fingers, these were cut off for purchase." Sharks feasted on the remains for several days afterward.[17]

We will never know the cause of the explosion. Most likely, a drunken sailor poked his candle through the magazine door or dropped pipe ashes where he shouldn't have. Morgan said his French prisoners had committed mass suicide rather than face trial for piracy. But he had no way of knowing that, since they all died.

Spaniards viewed the explosion as a miracle. At Cartagena, news of the disaster filled the churches with grateful citizens. Special thanks went to Nuestra Señora de la Popa, the city's patron saint. According to popular belief, "Our Lady's" statue often came to life after the sun set. On certain nights, the holy woman left her shrine in a monastery to search for Protestant raiders. She usually came back in the morning with her clothes muddy from walking in the jungle. On the morning after *Oxford* exploded, however, she returned wet and covered with seaweed—or so Cartagenians said.

They had good reason to be thankful. Losing *Oxford* forced Morgan to rethink his strategy. For one thing, he now lacked his other major ship. Fearing Spanish raids during his absence, Governor Modyford took *Satisfaction* away and sent it to patrol the coasts of Cuba and Hispaniola. Morgan moved his flag to the *Lilly*, a fifty-ton vessel mounting ten small guns. Worse, the accident cut the buccaneers' fighting strength nearly in half, forcing them to select an easier target. After another, less jolly meeting, they set sail for the Spanish Main. Destination: Maracaibo in present-day Venezuela.

Although hardly in the same class as Cartagena or Puerto Bello, this city of three thousand was still an attractive target. It lay on the western shore of the Laguna de Maracaibo, an immense freshwater lake fed by a network of rivers. Nowadays, the lake is the center of the Venezuelan oil industry. In Morgan's day, it was bordered by prosperous cattle ranches and plantations of cotton and tobacco. The area also held a special attraction for gold seekers. For over a century, Europeans believed that a fabulous kingdom lay in the jungle beyond the city of Maracaibo. Spaniards called it *La Tierra de Eldorado*, the Land of Eldorado.

They first heard of Eldorado in Mexico. After Hernán Cortés conquered the Aztecs in 1520, prisoners spoke of a tribe richer than any other. Although the Aztecs had always known about the tribe, no one had ever visited it; they knew only that it inhabited a sacred land deep in the jungles "to the south." Later, while searching for gold in Nicaragua, Costa Rica, and Panama, other conquistadores heard similar accounts. As always, Eldorado lay "further on." Native peoples may have believed the story; they may also have invented it to get rid of the white intruders as quickly as possible.

MORGAN'S MAJOR RAIDS 1663-1671

1663–65 Villahermosa, Grenada	——————
1668 Puerto Príncipe, Puerto Bello	··············
1668–69 Maracaibo	·–·–·–·–
1670–71 Panama	– – – – –

Map showing the routes of Henry Morgan's various buccaneering expeditions.

Spaniards learned that the land took its name from El Dorado, "The Gilded Man," a native king who was said to be half god and half man. El Dorado lived in a temple built of solid-gold bricks. Each spring, he led a procession to the shore of a lake for a solemn ceremony. Standing before his people, he removed his clothes and smeared his body with a paste of animal fat and gold dust. Accompanied by the sound of golden cymbals and trumpets, priests rowed him to the center of the lake. After saying a prayer, he plunged in and washed off the paste. At that very moment, the people ashore threw nuggets of pure gold, baskets of pearls, and handfuls of emeralds into the water. During countless centuries, the bottom of the lake became a carpet of gold and jewels.[18]

The land of Eldorado did not seem like a fairy tale to seventeenth-century Europeans. In the New World, truth often surpassed the strangest fiction. The conquistadores had made incredible discoveries in unlikely places. When, for example, Francisco Pizarro overthrew the Incan Empire in 1532, he found the *Coricancha* in Cuzco, their capital high in the Andes Mountains of Peru. The *Coricancha*, or "Golden Enclosure," was a garden set alongside a huge temple dedicated to the Incan sun god. Yet it was like no garden anywhere else in the world. Golden ears of corn hung from rows of golden plants, each tall as a man. Golden pebbles paved its walkways, and golden herdsmen watched over golden llamas, animals related to the camel. Golden butterflies perched on golden flowers, and golden spiders waited to snare golden crickets, all life-sized and exact down to the minutest detail. Thus, given Europeans' past experiences, the Gilded Man could easily have swum in Lake Maracaibo. Henry Morgan may or may not have believed the legend; many of his followers did. Whether the truth or not, he had everything to gain by visiting this area.

A narrow channel connected Lake Maracaibo to the sea. On the channel's lake side, several small islands, mere dots of land, lay behind a sandbar in shallow water. That pleased the buccaneers no end. Although their light craft could easily pass over the sandbar, it kept out the lumbering galleons. Nevertheless, Maracaibo's city fathers had not taken any chances. After a visit from the savage L'Olonnois, they built a castle on the Isla de San Carlos. Located atop a cliff overlooking the channel, this fortress was the city's only defense. If an invader could slip past it, he would

An anonymous Spanish artist depicts Indian priests sprinkling El Dorado, the Gilded Man, with gold dust.

have Maracaibo at his mercy. Despite his usual precautions, Morgan did not know about this dangerous obstacle.

The buccaneers reached the Venezuelan coast after sunset on March 9, 1669. Dousing the ships' lanterns, they furled their sails and coasted over the sandbar on the incoming tide. They anchored at the base of a cliff in a darkness so nearly total that they could barely see their hands in front of their faces, let alone the top of the cliff.

Dawn brought an unpleasant surprise. A stone castle crowned the cliff, its guns commanding the entrance to the lake. As long as the buccaneers hugged the shore, the Spaniards in the fortress could not depress their gun barrels enough to take aim. But if the buccaneers tried to sail further into the lake, or head back to the sea, the guns would blow them out of the water.

Morgan knew there was no point trying to wait out the defenders. Eventually, he would have to fight. So it might as well be now.

The buccaneers rowed to shore in longboats. Finding a disused path overgrown with weeds, they climbed for an hour and reached the top of the cliff. The castle lay before them, and they attacked in the usual way, with grapnels and grenadoes. After an all-day battle in which both sides took casualties, Morgan tried his favorite tactic—a surprise assault under cover of darkness. What he did not know was that the Spanish commander had anticipated his move. A sly fellow, after making certain preparations, he evacuated the garrison through a rear gate, leaving only one soldier behind. That man was unarmed, except for a piece of flint of the type used to start fires.

At Morgan's signal, the buccaneers charged the front gate. In their excitement, nobody realized that they were doing all the shooting. Bursting through the gate, they ran smack into a wall of—silence. Except for a few pack mules and some supplies stacked in neat piles, the castle seemed deserted. Spanish soldiers were nowhere to be seen, not even the soldier who had just slipped out the rear gate. The defenders had vanished without a trace. Without a fight!

The buccaneers milled about, not knowing what to make of this odd turn of events. Then they shot their muskets into the air and roared like wild men over a kill. They told each other that the Spaniards had snuck away. That was a good sign, a wonderful sign! It meant that, from then on, they could expect smooth sail-

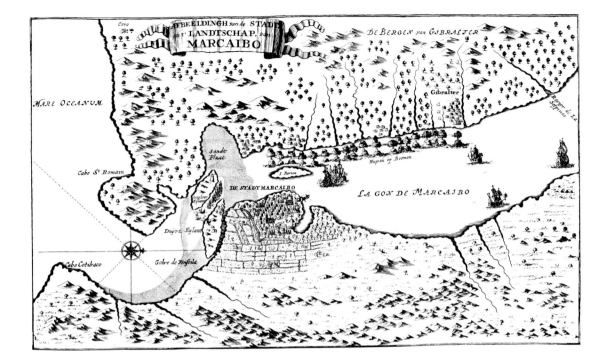

Map of the entrance to
Lake Maracaibo from
the Dutch edition of
Esquemeling's *The
Buccaneers of America.*

ing. Even if they did not find the treasures of El Dorado, Maracaibo lay at their feet, ready for looting. Already they could see themselves drinking in the taverns of Port Royal.

Their chief felt uneasy. He had taken the castle too easily. Why? The answer came ringing like an alarm bell. The Spaniards had *given* him the place.

The luck that had saved him from death aboard the *Oxford* seemed still to hold. Crinkling his nostrils, Morgan smelled trouble—literally. It came as a wisp of acrid smoke. He had smelled that particular kind of smoke countless times. It came from a rope match! Somewhere nearby a rope match was smoldering.

Morgan followed the smell and, sure enough, found a fuse leading into the castle's magazine. The Spanish soldier had cut it to burn for fifteen minutes, and the flame was just two feet away from a pile of gunpowder barrels. The castle was a bomb set to explode! With only seconds to spare, Morgan stamped out the fuse.

What should he do about the castle? The wisest move would be to occupy it and hold the channel against any Spanish relief force. But that would take at least fifty men, far more than he could spare. So Morgan did the next best thing. He ordered the castle's guns thrown from the walls and spiked; that is, made useless by hammering a large nail into the firing mechanism. To use the guns again, the Spaniards would have to drill out the nails, a long and difficult job. Morgan failed to take the added precaution of blowing up the walls, an error he would later regret. Instead, he took the Spanish gunpowder and set sail.

The buccaneers entered the lake and headed for their objective, Maracaibo. Again they met a wall of silence. "The towne at our arrival wee found quitted," Morgan wrote in his official report.[19] News of the castle's fall had traveled faster than his ships. Except for a handful of people too ill to be moved, Maracaibo was deserted. Everyone else had loaded pack mules with food and fled into the jungle with their valuables. These "valuables" included scores of black slaves.

Morgan gave the refugees no rest. While most of his men searched the town, the rest scoured the countryside for prisoners. Spaniards who had not fled far enough now had to take their turn with the torturers. Besides the usual cruelties, Esquemeling describes how captives were "crucified . . . and with kindled matches were burnt between their fingers and toes. Others had their feet put into the fire, and thus were left to be roasted alive."[20] After three weeks of nonstop terrorism, Morgan realized that he had picked Maracaibo clean. Instead of turning back, however, he decided to capture Gibraltar at the southern end of the lake. "Gibraltore," as he called it, was a prosperous town of about fifteen hundred inhabitants.

His ships anchored six miles from Gibraltar. An advance party went the rest of the way with twelve prisoners. Morgan promised the prisoners freedom in return for delivering his usual message: Unless the citizens of Gibraltar surrendered without a fight, he vowed to kill them all and bury their remains under the town's ashes.

Again Spanish civilians fled into the jungle in terror. And again the buccaneers looted and searched for captives to torture. They had the help of a man they tempted with freedom and then turned into a murderer. Esquemeling says they "found a certain slave, unto whom they promised mountains of gold and that they would give him his liberty by transporting him unto Jamaica, in case he would show them the places where the inhabitants of Gibraltar lay hidden. The fellow conducted them unto a party of Spaniards, whom they instantly made all prisoners, commanding the said slave to kill some of them before the eyes of the rest; to the intent that by this perpetrated crime he might never be able to leave their . . . company."[21] In effect, the slave traded one type of bondage for another. Having killed Spaniards, he could never be safe except with the buccaneers.

Gibraltar's reign of terror lasted five weeks. Satisfied at last, Morgan loaded the booty aboard his ships and returned to Maracaibo. Things were as he had left them. Apart from an old man who had returned to his house, the town lay silent and deserted. From him Morgan learned that Spanish warships had arrived on the coast a few days earlier.

Alarmed at this turn of events, he sent his fastest ship to scout the area and report back within twenty-four hours. Sure enough, the old man had told the truth. Three galleons rode at anchor on the Caribbean side of the sandbar, blocking the channel to the sea, yet unable to enter the lake. Each galleon had enough fire-power to blast Morgan's entire fleet out of the water. To make matters worse, soldiers had occupied the castle and replaced its guns with heavier ones from their ships. The invaders were trapped.

Morgan sent a prisoner with a message for the Spanish commander. Most men in his position would have asked for surrender terms. Not the buccaneer chief. Brash as ever, he demanded a safe-conduct for his fleet and a large sum of money as the price for not burning Maracaibo.

The prisoner returned with a letter, dated April 24, 1669, from Admiral Alonso del Campo y Espinosa. A brave yet cautious man, Don Alonso did not want to fight unless absolutely necessary. "My intent is to dispute with you your passage out of the lake, and follow and pursue you everywhere," wrote the admiral. "Notwithstanding, if you be contented to surrender with humility all you have taken, together with the slaves and all other prisoners, I will let you freely pass, without trouble or molestation; upon condition that you retire presently unto your own country." Should Morgan offer resistance, Don Alonso promised to send for smaller vessels to carry his soldiers over the sandbar. "They will cause you utterly to perish, by putting every man to the sword. . . . I have with me excellent soldiers, who desire nothing more ardently than to revenge on you and your people all the cruelties and base infamous actions you have committed upon the Spanish nation in America."[22]

Morgan had not come to "Marracaia," as he called the place,

to surrender with humility. Nor had he come to perish. His reply to Don Alonso's letter was itself a challenge. "Sir," he declared, "I shall save you ye labour . . . to come here, being resolved to visit you with all expedition, and there wee will putt to hazard of Battle in whose power it shall be to use clemency (yours wee are acquainted with nor doe wee expect any.)"[23]

Later that day, Morgan gathered the buccaneers in Maracaibo's main square. What followed was the finest performance of his life. We say "performance," because, like a skilled actor, he intended every word and gesture to have an effect upon his audience.

He did not try to hide the facts; indeed, he painted a very gloomy picture. Yes, they were trapped, outnumbered, and outgunned, he said. And, yes, he promised to abide by whatever his buccaneers decided in an open vote. Before voting, however, he wanted them to answer some questions. Did they wish to escape by surrendering everything they had "purchased" over the last two months? They also knew the Spaniards; they had been fighting them for years. Now, what faith could they have in the word of a Spanish admiral? Had not Don Alonso mentioned buccaneer "cruelties" and "infamous actions" in his letter? Once they laid down their weapons, would he not be as merciless to them as they had been to captured Spaniards?

There was no need for discussion. The answers were self-evident. When Morgan finished, his men shouted their defiance. "They had rather fight and spill the last drop of the blood they had in their veins," Esquemeling recalled, "than surrender so easily the booty they had gotten with so much danger to their lives."[24]

That was exactly the result Morgan had sought to achieve. Raising his hand for silence, he proposed a plan—a surefire plan, with the emphasis on "fire." He wanted the carpenters to build a *brûlot*. The word comes from the French *brûler*, "to burn." A *brûlot* was a fireship, a device as old as war at sea. Fire, as we have seen, was the sailing ship's deadliest enemy. Sir Francis Drake had used history's most famous fireships eighty-one years earlier. In August 1588, they had played a key role in the defeat of the "Invincible Armada," a huge Spanish fleet sent to conquer England.

Everyone liked the chief's idea. Immediately after the vote, work began on a small ship captured at Gibraltar. Carpenters buried its lower deck with anything that could burn—tar, pitch, loose gunpowder—and covered it with dry leaves and branches. At key points they placed kegs of gunpowder joined by short fuses ready for ignition. With crowbars they loosened timbers above the waterline, so that the force of the explosion would more easily shatter the hull. Logs painted to resemble cannons lined the main deck; a keg of gunpowder and a pile of cannonballs lay beside each "gun." Finally, as a whimsical touch, they made dozens of figures out of wood and straw-filled sacks. Each figure wore buccaneer clothes, had a painted face, and held a musket. The *brûlot*'s only genuine crewmen were twelve volunteers with a special mission. A longboat bobbed in the water behind the fireship, attached to its stern by a rope. Once the twelve men accomplished their mission, only the longboat stood between them and certain death.

Meantime, a black man serving as a spy came aboard Don Alonso's galleon, the forty-gun *Magdalena*, with vital information. "Sir," he told the admiral, "be pleased to have great care of yourself, for the English have prepared a fireship with desire to burn your fleet."[25]

Don Alonso did not appreciate the warning. "How can that be?" he snorted. "Have they wit enough to build a fireship? Or what instruments have they to do it?"[26] The proud Spaniard refused to credit the buccaneers with enough intelligence to build such a destructive device. Nevertheless, one could not be too careful with the likes of Henry Morgan. So, as an added precaution, he had water barrels placed every few feet on his ships' decks.

After that, six days passed without either side making a move. Toward evening of the sixth day, April 30, Morgan's fleet left Maracaibo in line-ahead formation; that is, each vessel sailing about fifty yards behind the other. The *brûlot* took the lead, followed by five smaller vessels loaded with fighting men. The three largest vessels, including Morgan's *Lilly*, came up the rear with the prisoners and booty. Meanwhile, the Spaniards opened their gun ports and waited for the buccaneers to get closer. But since it was nearly dark, Morgan ordered a halt for the night. Nevertheless, he did not want the Spaniards to get the wrong idea. To show that he meant to fight, he kept the ships' lanterns lit.

Sunrise. May 1, 1669. May Day. Morgan gave the order to weigh anchor and head straight for the galleons.

Don Alonso bolted from his cabin, shouting orders as he ran to his post on *Magdalena*'s quarterdeck.

The buccaneers came on boldly, clearly intending to hurl their grapnels and board. The Spanish admiral, however, had anticipated this move. Dozens of sailors waited in *Magdalena*'s rigging, ready to leap onto the enemy's deck with cutlasses and pistols. Meanwhile, helmsmen strained against the great wheels, slowly turning the galleons broadside to the oncoming enemy. How perfect! How beautiful!, Don Alonso thought. There, before his very eyes, was a sea-fighter's dream come true. His guns were about to blow *los diablos Ingleses*, those English devils, to smithereens.

"Ahora! Fiero!" "Now! Fire!"

Three galleons opened fire at the same moment. Solid shot whizzed overhead, shredding the fireship's sails. Geysers erupted in its path and on either side of its bow. Still, a miss is as good as a mile. The fireship slid across the sandbar and kept coming, straight as an arrow.

Her crew of twelve saw the galleons grow larger by the minute. Suddenly the sea artist veered to the right, aiming to hit *Magdalena* amidships, just as his chief planned. By destroying her, Morgan hoped to give his other vessels a chance to board her sister ships in the confusion.

The fireship slammed into *Magdalena*'s side with a teeth-rattling *crunch*. Instantly grapnels came hurtling through the air, hooked onto her railings, and held fast. Instantly boarders leapt onto the intruder's deck from *Magdalena*'s rigging. They met no resistance. Save for its savage-looking scarecrows, the vessel was deserted. What the Spaniards did not notice was the twelve-man crew furiously rowing away. Before leaving, they had lit the fuses belowdecks.

Moments later, boarders saw tongues of flame licking through cracks in the planking beneath their feet. Fanned by a stiff breeze, the separate fires merged into a single, all-consuming inferno. The vessel—hull, masts, yardarms, decks—blazed from stem to stern. Her torn sails ignited, turning the shrouds into filaments of fire. Black gobs of bubbling, hissing tar oozed along her decks and down her sides. The deck guns, loaded with solid shot, fired in the intense heat.

The flames spread so quickly that few boarders had time to

leap over the side. And, hard as they tried, *Magdalena*'s crew could not push that devil ship away or undo the grapnels. Held in an unbreakable death grip, the galleon also caught fire. Moments later, flames reached the fireship's gunpowder kegs and both vessels erupted in a clap of thunder.

Next thing he knew, Don Alonso was tumbling through the air like a rag doll flung by an angry child. He came down with a painful *slap*, amid mangled corpses and living men clinging to floating wreckage. The shock of the cool water cleared his head and he kicked off his boots. Then he swam toward shore.

Panic reigned aboard the other galleons. Believing everything lost, the captain of the *Santa Louisa* ran his thirty-gun vessel onto the beach below the castle and took refuge behind its walls. Morgan's five fighting ships came over the sandbar to attack *La Marquesa*, the third galleon, capturing her after a short, sharp fight. Morgan took her as his flagship.

Esquemeling describes his comrades as "extremely gladdened at this signal victory, obtained in so short a time and with so great inequality of forces; whereby they contrived greater pride in their minds than they had before."[27] Their mood changed, however, when they looked toward the top of the cliff. The castle's guns still commanded the exit to the sea. Shaken but determined to have his revenge, Don Alonso had taken control of them. The buccaneers were still trapped.

Again Morgan showed daring and imagination. Problem: How could eight slow-moving vessels pass beneath those guns without being destroyed? Answer: Persuade the enemy to take the guns away. Morgan put himself in Don Alonso's place. The Spaniard, he believed, expected him to attack the castle next. Very well. He would pretend to do as expected, then escape.

Next day, the buccaneers awoke early. Under Don Alonso's

The Spanish Armada destroyed by Captaine Morgan

very eyes, longboats filled with armed men pushed away from the ships and headed for a wooded area along the shore. Although the Spaniards could not see them after they reached their destination, they could still count. All day, the boats ferried men to the landing place, always returning "empty" except for the oarsmen. Obviously, hundreds of buccaneers were getting into position for a night attack on the castle's undefended, or land, side.

They were doing nothing of the sort. Morgan had ordered most of his men to stay belowdecks, out of sight. Only a handful actually went into the longboats. However, instead of going ashore, they lay flat in the boats for the return ride. The Spaniards only saw the longboats heading for the ships' port

The buccaneer fleet escapes from Lake Maracaibo. From the Spanish edition of Esquemeling's *The Buccaneers of America.*

sides, which faced away from the castle. Next time the longboats appeared, they were filled again—with the same men.

Don Alonso swallowed the bait. He ordered the guns moved from the castle's lake side to its land side.

Night came, a glorious tropical night with a starry sky and the moon hanging like a golden lantern. The Spaniards waited anxiously for the usual salvo of musket balls announcing a buccaneer assault. It never came.

What followed next was entirely unexpected. A lookout noticed dark shapes moving on the lake, directly in front of the castle. *"Los Ingleses!"* he shouted. The buccaneer fleet was gliding down the channel on the outgoing tide! The Spaniards managed to haul a few guns back into position, but too late to do any good.

A happy Henry Morgan stood on deck. He had won after all. As a final insult, he "saluted" the castle with some parting cannon shots. The buccaneers reached Port Royal on May 27 with booty valued at 250,000 pieces of eight, besides scores of black slaves and white prisoners unable to pay their ransom. Morgan promptly sold all of them into bondage.

Four
The Flames of Panama

"Thus was consumed that famous and ancient City of Panama, which is the greatest Mart for Silver and Gold in the whole World."
—Henry Morgan to Sir Thomas Modyford, April 20, 1671

Puerto Príncipe. Puerto Bello. Maracaibo. Gibraltar. How romantic those names sounded to those who lived under England's weeping skies! Although most of Henry Morgan's countrymen could scarcely pronounce these names, much less find them on a map, news of the buccaneer's exploits came across the ocean like rays of warming sunshine.

English people desperately needed cheering up in 1669. Few years within living memory had been gloomier than the previous ones. Disaster had followed disaster in rapid succession. In 1665, an epidemic of bubonic plague carried off thirty thousand people in London alone. Writers could scarcely find words to describe the horror. Every evening burial carts rolled down cobblestone streets, their drivers' mournful cries echoing through deserted streets: "Bring out your dead!" And every evening scores of Londoners carried out loved ones who had died during the day.

Gravediggers buried the bodies in long trenches outside the city.

No sooner did the Great Plague subside when the Great Fire of London came in 1666. The inferno raged for five days, consuming over thirteen thousand buildings and leaving half the population homeless. "It made me weep to see it," a government official wrote in his diary. "The churches, houses, and all on fire and flaming at once, and a horrid noise the flames made, and of cracking of the houses at their ruin."[1] To add insult to injury, in 1667 the Royal Navy suffered a humiliating defeat during a brief war with the Netherlands. A Dutch battle fleet sailed up the Thames River and sank some of England's finest warships as they rode at anchor. For English people, therefore, Morgan's victories over the old enemy, Spain, raised their spirits during a dismal time.

Morgan's victims, however, saw things differently. To them, he was simply a thief and a murderer. Count de Molina, the Spanish ambassador, protested after each raid in the strongest terms. His Excellency reminded English diplomats that their countries had signed a peace treaty when King Charles II came to the throne in 1660. Count de Molina demanded that the government punish the buccaneer and his accomplice, Sir Thomas Modyford, and return their "purchase" to its rightful owners.

English diplomats replied by reading a list of their country's grievances. They reminded His Excellency of the longstanding rule: "Beyond the Line no other rule is recognized but that of force."[2] The peace treaty applied only to Europe, they insisted. If Spain wanted an end to privateering, let her open her colonial ports to English trade, stop molesting honest merchants, and leave Jamaica alone.

Count Molina cut them short with a wave of his hand. Such

demands, he snapped, were the same as asking for his master's eyes, ears, and tongue. No king of Spain could yield on such basic principles. Spain would rather fight than yield to blackmail.

King Charles did not want to push Spain too hard. Although England and Holland soon made peace, everyone knew it could not last; the war might resume at any moment. Since it made no sense to fight both Spain and Holland, His Majesty ordered Governor Modyford to cancel all privateering commissions as a sign of England's good faith. Sir Thomas, however, did not think the Spanish leopard had changed its spots. Spain, he wrote, still meant to drive the English from the West Indies. Yet orders are orders. In the fall of 1669, he ended Jamaican privateering.

Ending privateering, however, raised another question. What to do about the buccaneers? These men lived by robbery and brutality. If they could not rob Spaniards legally, they might turn pirate and rob everyone. Sir Thomas could not allow that to happen. Nor could he deprive Jamaica of its only defenders.

The governor decided to wait patiently. Time was on his side, he believed. Eventually Spain would provoke an incident, allowing him to strike back in "self-defense." Until then, he must keep the buccaneers out of trouble yet also retain their loyalty. That would not be easy. He had to use the utmost tact, getting his meaning across while leaving certain things unsaid. If he said too much, enemies might later use his words against him. More than one English politician had lost his head for saying the wrong thing at the wrong time.

Sir Thomas met privately with the buccaneer chief. "I should be happy to be able to write His Majesty how well your plantation was doing under your own skillful attention," he said. "He would be very glad indeed to hear that you and your good wife were enjoying its peace and comforts together."[3] *Your own skilled attention!* Translation: Morgan must stay out of sight for a while, preferably away from Port Royal, and persuade his followers to do the same.

The buccaneer agreed. Perhaps the matter did need his personal attention—for a while. *For a while!* Translation: Morgan agreed to set an example. He would lay low, keeping his sword sharp and his pistols loaded until the right time came. Hopefully, it would come sooner rather than later.[4]

Before long, Sir Thomas could write His Majesty that things were proceeding splendidly in Jamaica. Morgan had settled into the dull, though respectable, life of a planter. So had his captains, who were investing their prize money in land and slaves. Although some buccaneers turned pirate, the majority became merchants, trading with the settlements along the Spanish Main, or returned to the hunting camps in Hispaniola.

Yet, as the governor predicted, it did not last. Morgan's raids had shocked Spain to the core. Hurt and humiliated by his arrogance, she launched open warfare across the Line. The government raised taxes to pay for fresh troops and supplies. Six new galleons went on patrol duty in the Caribbean. Colonial governors received orders to attack every English ship, island, and port in the West Indies. To help in the "sacred undertaking," they might issue letters of marque and reprisal. Privateering could cut both ways. Now let the English have a taste of their own medicine!

Fighting began in Cuban waters late in January 1670. A certain Captain Barnard, or Bart, had taken the *Mary and Jane* from Port Royal to the port of Manzanillo with a cargo of English trade goods. The settlers, as usual, bought everything. Town officials, as usual, took their bribes and turned a blind eye. Everyone was satisfied.

A few hours after leaving Manzanillo, a lookout aboard *Mary and Jane* sighted a vessel in the distance. Since she flew an English flag, Captain Barnard shortened sail, allowing her to catch up. This was not unusual; friendly ships often "spoke" to one another—exchanged information—upon meeting at sea.

This stranger, however, had used a pirate trick to make her approach. Coming within range, she "showed her true colors." Suddenly the English flag fluttered down and the colors of Spain rose to the masthead. "Defend yourself, dog," a voice boomed across the water in perfect English. "I come as a punishment for heretics."[5] With that, the stranger's gun ports flew open and she began firing. The first volley swept across *Mary and Jane*'s deck, toppling her mainmast and blowing Captain Barnard into shapeless lumps of flesh and bone. Seeing their captain dead and their ship a mass of flames, the crew surrendered.

The attacker was the *San Pedro y la Fama*, captained by Manuel Rivera Pardal, a ten-gun privateer out of Santiago de Cuba. Little is known of Captain Pardal except that he spoke English and had vowed to become the Spanish Henry Morgan. Encouraged by this "victory," Pardal attacked Jamaica itself. In June, he raided along the island's northern coast, burning settlements and seizing both whites and blacks as slaves. Although Pardal took little money, he gave the Jamaicans an awful scare. His raids, they feared, were just the beginning. The nearest part of Cuba is less than one hundred miles from the Jamaican coast. Using Cuba as a jump-off point, Spanish troops could come ashore and wage guerrilla warfare from the mountains, just as the buccaneers had done in Hispaniola.

Pardal's success went to his head. Toward the end of June, he landed fifty miles from Port Royal, burned several houses, and nailed a message to a palm tree. After boasting of his achievements, Pardal revealed his true purpose: "I am come to seek Admiral Morgan, with two ships of war, and having seen this, I crave he would come out upon the coast and seek me, that he might see the valor of the Spaniards."[6] Like a Western gunfighter "calling out" the best shot in town, Pardal hoped to make his reputation by defeating the buccaneer chief. Killing Morgan would make him the most feared person in the West Indies. Spain would then do anything, pay anything, to have him on its side. Why, he might become the governor of a colony, even a "son of someone." The possibilities were endless, at least in his vivid imagination.

The challenge backfired. It made Pardal's intended victim the most important person on the island. To his fellow Jamaicans, Henry Morgan was now their natural leader, their savior, more important than the governor himself. He alone stood between them and the "Spanish fury."

Events began to move with dizzying speed. On June 29, two days after receiving Pardal's challenge, Sir Thomas Modyford held an emergency meeting of the Council of Jamaica. Composed of the island's most powerful men, this body advised the governor on all vital questions.

As the council members gathered, word came that Pardal was not the only captain operating under Spanish privateering commissions. A ship had arrived that very day with documents taken from another Spanish privateer and news that war had been declared in Cartagena. Given these facts, the council passed a unanimous resolution. Jamaica was in grave danger, the resolution said. Only the buccaneers and their chief could save the island.

Sir Thomas must put Morgan in charge of Jamaica's defenses—
ships, sailors, soldiers, civilian volunteers—and turn him loose on
the enemy.

The governor agreed. On July 2, Port Royal's town crier proclaimed war against the Spanish colonies by land and sea, by fire
and sword. On July 22, Sir Thomas sent written instructions to
"Admiral Henry Morgan, Esquire." The instructions commanded
him to raise a strike force "on the old pleasing account of no purchase no pay."

Sir Thomas did not limit Morgan's activities to the defense of
Jamaica. He allowed the "admiral" to attack Spaniards anywhere
he found them and by any means. Not only must the buccaneer
chief upset their invasion plans, but he must ignite slave rebellions in their colonies. Such rebellions might result in the massacre of innocent people, but if it took that to save Jamaica, then
so be it. After landing in Spanish territory, Morgan should offer
protection to any settlers who declared their loyalty to King
Charles. In addition, he must "proclaim . . . liberty to all the
slaves that will come in; and give notice that their fugitive masters'
plantations are to be divided amongst them as rewards & make
them sufficient grants in writing, both for their liberties and es-
tates."[7] Morgan was the first English commander to receive such
broad authority, but not the last. During the American Revolution
and War of 1812, English generals promised slaves freedom in return for fighting against their masters. These masters included
men such as George Washington, Thomas Jefferson, and Andrew
Jackson.

The commission concluded with a brutal kill order. If
Spaniards and slaves refused to listen to reason, "you are then,
with all expedition to destroy and burn all habitations, and leave

it as a wilderness, putting the men-slaves to the sword and making the women-slaves prisoners to be brought hither, and sold." Morgan must also discover how the local people treated English prisoners, "and being well informed, you are to give the same"; that is, treat Spanish prisoners in the same manner, allowing both kindness and terror to teach by example. Last but not least, the admiral received authority to "do all manner of exploits"; that is, *anything* he thought necessary for the success of his mission.[8]

On August 14, 1670, Morgan sailed from Port Royal, anchoring off Cow Island three days later. Before leaving, however, he called for men and ships to help deliver the most devastating blow ever struck by the Brethren of the Coast.

His reputation for success drew the Brethren like sharks to blood. Nothing like it had ever been seen in the West Indies. Rugged sea rovers came in barques and brigs, sleek two-masted vessels able to sail rings around any galleon. Many others turned up in tiny open boats, canoes, even rafts that wallowed in the swells. Their crews "boxed the compass"—came from all directions—lured by promises of adventure, revenge, and booty. English buccaneers from Jamaica, the majority, rubbed shoulders with hard-faced men from Massachusetts and Virginia. Frenchmen came from Tortuga, and Dutchmen from Nieu Amsterdam, as they still called New York (conquered by England in 1664). Bands of hunters hailed passing ships from jungle-fringed beaches. Juan de Lao, an Indian cook, described the only female buccaneer: "She was small and old and English, and it was publicly said that she was a witch whom the English had brought along to prophesy for them and through her diabolical arts to advise them what they should do."[9]

Henry Morgan needed no witchcraft to tell him what to do.

While the fleet assembled, he sent raiders to Hispaniola and Cuba to seize supplies. Among them was the *Dolphin*, commanded by Captain John Morris, a veteran buccaneer and Morgan's most trusted aide. One day in November, the *Dolphin* ran into a storm off Cuba's eastern coast. Blown into a sheltered bay, she found Manuel Pardal's ship riding at anchor. In the battle that followed, the Spanish privateer fell dead with a bullet in the neck. His crew surrendered, giving Morgan a fine ship for his fleet.

On December 2, a war council met aboard the *Satisfaction*, recently returned from patrol duty. Where should they strike? The captains mentioned four possibilities: Santiago de Cuba, Cuba's second city after Havana; Vera Cruz, New Spain's chief seaport; Cartagena, capital of the Spanish Main; and the city of Panama. After much discussion, they ruled out the first three. That left Panama, Morgan's objective from the beginning. He had not forgotten his promise to Don Augustín de Bracamonte at Puerto Bello. Well, time had run out. Proud "Penamaw," as he called it, was about to feel the heavy hand of war.

The story of Panama began in 1513. After weeks of trudging through steaming jungle, a Spanish explorer, Vasco Núñez de Balboa, stood on a hilltop overlooking a mighty ocean. Although Europeans had approached this ocean from the east, by sailing around Africa, Balboa was the first white person to see the Pacific from the west. Deeply moved, the explorer put on a suit of armor and ran downhill, through an Indian village built along the shore. With a sword in one hand and a flag in the other, Balboa waded into the surf to claim all lands it touched for Spain. Six years later, his countrymen began building a city on the site of the Indian village. They called it by its Indian name, *Panama,* or "place of good fishing." Panama was already one hundred five years old when Pieter Minuit bought Manhattan Island from the Indians.

The city lay at the narrowest part of what we now call the Isthmus of Panama. An isthmus is a narrow strip of land connecting two larger landmasses bordered on either side by a large body of water—in this case by the Caribbean Sea and Pacific Ocean. Within a few years, vast amounts of treasure began to move across the isthmus, making the city one of the wealthiest in the world. Its full name tells just how much Spaniards prized it: *El Muy Noble y Muy Leal Ciudad de Panama*, The Very Noble and Very Loyal City of Panama.

In approaching Panama from the east, travelers crossed the Plain of Matasnillos, a rolling grassland broken by low hills and shady valleys dotted with orchards and cattle ranches. Seen from the distance, Panama was a gorgeous city of red-tiled roofs stretching for nearly a mile along the Pacific shore. By the late 1600s, it had a population of between seven and ten thousand, of whom at least half were people of color: Africans; mulattoes (persons of mixed black and white parentage); and *zambos,* which is the Spanish term for the descendants of blacks and Indians. Members of the last two groups were free, if their mothers had been born free. Africans, however, were slaves. Panama was *the* slave market of the Spanish Empire. The city supplied slaves to every colony from Peru to New Spain. Panama's slave traders kept their human "stock" in acres of iron-and-wood cages until they went to the auction block.

Panama had seven thousand houses. These included scores of elegant mansions belonging to the wealthiest merchants and highest government officials. Such houses would have been the pride of any city in Spain. Built of polished stone, they had silken

Ruins of the steeple of the Cathedral of Saint Anastasius, Old Panama, as they existed about the year 1900.

curtains, ornate tapestries, and elegant furniture imported from the mother country. Rich men's houses often had rooms resembling jewel boxes lined with sweet-smelling rosewood. The ceilings were often painted with Spanish country scenes.

No white resident of Panama could be described as poor, only less wealthy. Ordinary Spaniards lived in solid wooden houses built around gardens for shade and privacy. These people made their living from trade, agriculture, and pearl fishing at a group of islands called, naturally, the Pearl Islands.

In gratitude for God's blessings, Panamanians built seven monasteries, eight churches, and a cathedral dedicated to Saint Anastasius. These houses of God contained saints' statues made of precious metals studded with jewels. The cathedral, however, outshone them all. So high was its tower that Indians believed angels leaned down from heaven to ring its bells. Inside, it had a high altar covered with thick plates of solid gold. A life-size statue of the Virgin Mary wore a silk robe embroidered with gold thread. Candles in gold and silver candlesticks bathed everything in a shimmering light that seemed to come from heaven; visitors said that passing through the massive wooden doors was like stepping into a treasure chest.

Father Thomas Gage had visited Panama in the 1620s, but things had not changed very much over the next fifty years. The "best" people paraded their wealth for fellow citizens to admire. "The gentlemen have their train of . . . slaves, some a dozen, some a half dozen, waiting on them, in brave, gallant [clothes], heavy with gold and silver lace, with silk stockings on their black legs, and roses on their feet, and swords by their sides. The ladies also carry their train by their coach's side [and are served by] . . . jet-like damsels . . . in light apparel, who with their bravery and white mantles over them seem to be, as the Spaniard saith, 'mosca en leche,' a fly in milk."[10]

Yet living in Panama had drawbacks even for the wealthy. Although the climate was not as deadly as Puerto Bello's, the city sweltered in heat and humidity the year round. An anonymous visitor noted that the streets ran east and west, the worst layout possible. Thus, "when the sun rises no one can walk in any of the streets, because there is no shade whatever; and this is felt very much as the heat is intense; and the sun is so prejudicial to health, that if a man is exposed to its rays for a few hours, he will be attacked by a fatal fever, and this has happened to many." The harbor made matters worse, thanks to the great rise and fall of the tides. To reach the shore at low tide, one had to walk for almost a mile over foul-smelling black mud. "At full moon," the visitor added, "the waves frequently reach the houses and enter those on that side of town."[11]

Panama's citizens shrugged their shoulders at reports from Puerto Bello and other places. It was too bad, of course, that Morgan's villains had pillaged those cities, but really none of their concern. They had good reason to feel immune from such misfortunes. One side of their city rested on the shore of the Pacific, virtually a Spanish lake. Except for a brush with Sir Francis Drake's *Golden Hind* in 1578, no enemy vessel had ever come close to attacking Panama. On the Caribbean side of the isthmus, the Chagres River offered the easiest route cross-country, except for the castle guarding its mouth. Panama's main defense, however, was the isthmus itself. Only sixty miles from coast to coast, it challenged invaders with some of the roughest country in the New World: jungle, swamps, quicksand, mountains. If the buccaneers felt like tackling these, then let them come!

While Panamanians went about their affairs, Henry Morgan made his final preparations. Since he expected heavy fighting, he drew up a new set of articles. These allowed more money for each type of wound, with one exception: the loss of an eye. In addition, the articles provided bonuses for bravery above and beyond the call of duty. For example, the first buccaneer to fight his way into a castle could claim an extra fifty pieces of eight. The buccaneer who hauled down a Spanish flag and raised the English flag would receive a purse full of doubloons.

On December 8, 1670, Morgan gave the signal to weigh anchor. He left Cow Island with 1,846 men aboard thirty-six ships, of which twenty-eight were English. Besides the *Satisfaction*, three ships bore the name *Fortune* and two *Prosperous*, possibly in expectation of future profits. Other vessels had names like *Port Royal*, *Virgin Queen*, *The Gift*, *The Free Gift*, *Mayflower*, and *Recovery*. They ranged in size from 12 to 120 tons, and carried a total of 239 guns, or the equivalent of three large galleons. Although small by European standards, Morgan's force was huge for the West Indies, a tribute to him personally and the high point of his career as a buccaneer. Thanks to his leadership and reputation, nearly every English and French buccaneer had joined under a single command. They did not know it then, but far away in Madrid, Spain, diplomats had recently signed a treaty to sweep buccaneers from the Caribbean.

Morgan set a course for Santa Catalina island, arriving there six days later. Located just 250 miles from the coast of Panama, this ten square miles of sand and brush was actually two islands: Santa Catalina itself and Isla Chica, Little Island, joined to it by a narrow sliver of land. Santa Catalina had several farms and a convict settlement guarded by soldiers. Isla Chica had a strong fort on a hill overlooking a fine bay. Although the place had little value in itself, Morgan had a special reason for his visit: information.[12]

He landed on Santa Catalina with a thousand men; that is, five times the Spanish force. Nevertheless, the defenders had the upper hand. Safe in their fort, they pounded the island with solid shot. After a day of ducking and dodging, the buccaneers settled down to a night of misery. Expecting to help themselves to Spanish provisions, they had left their food aboard the ships. Thus, only a lucky few found anything to eat—an old horse "both lean and full of scabs and blotches."[13] Rain began to fall after midnight, soaking them and ending any hope of sleep. The downpour continued without letup the next day, encouraging talk of mutiny. Morgan responded in his usual way. He sent the Spaniards an ultimatum: surrender or he would "put them all to the sword."[14] It was a bluff, but he counted on his reputation for terrorism to weaken their will to resist.

The threat worked. Within an hour, a messenger came from the Spanish commander. He carried the strangest request Morgan had ever received. Yes, the man said, his master would give up, provided Morgan allowed him to do so in the "proper" way. Shyly, almost apologetically, he explained the situation. His master wished to save both his honor and his skin. Surrendering without a fight, he knew, meant a trial for cowardice and a hangman's rope. The only solution, therefore, was to stage a farce rather than a battle. The commander wanted Morgan to "attack" with every man and gun at his disposal. There must be plenty of noise and heavy firing on both sides, only everyone would shoot cannons without cannonballs. Thus the commander could tell his superiors that he had surrendered only after a gallant struggle against overwhelming odds.

Morgan put on a grand display. That night, his ships turned broadside to the fort and opened fire. Oh, how awesome! How magnificent! Orange gunflashes pierced the darkness. The vibrations of the big guns punched crewmen in the ears like hard fists, sounding like the crack of doom. Clouds of burnt gunpowder enveloped the ships and drifted across the bay. Meanwhile, landing parties charged the fort, shouting and shooting every step of the way. Cheering Spaniards answered in kind.

Peering through the smoke, Morgan caught glimpses of a white flag flying from the fort. Nobody died. The only blood shed was that of an enthusiastic Frenchman who stumbled and nearly beheaded himself with his own cutlass. His comrades celebrated by wolfing down the Spaniards' food and draining their wine barrels.

Their chief found exactly what he had come for: three convicts who were familiar with the Isthmus of Panama. Their names and nationality are unknown; they could just as easily have been Spaniards as Englishmen or Frenchmen. What is certain is that, in return for guiding his army, Morgan promised them double shares. Then he spiked the fort's guns, loaded fifteen tons of Spanish gunpowder aboard his ships, and set sail. He did not garrison the fort, guessing (correctly) that the Spaniards would soon be too busy to think about retaking it.

Captain Joseph Bradley of the *Mayflower* went ahead with 470 men in three ships. One of Morgan's most trusted aides, Bradley had an important mission. Not only must he capture El Castillo de San Lorenzo de Chagres and secure the river's mouth before the main force arrived, but he must do it before news of the invasion reached Panama. His chief, as usual, hoped to catch the enemy by surprise.

Bradley arrived on the morning of January 5, 1671. Viewing San Lorenzo through a telescope, he realized that it would be a hard nut to crack. Manned by 350 hand-picked soldiers and a squad of Indian archers, the fortress crowned a barren hilltop on the river's eastern bank. The hill had twin peaks separated by a deep ravine spanned by a drawbridge that led to the main gate.

The castle itself lay behind a double wall of wooden planks, placed six feet apart, and the space between filled with earth; this could absorb any cannonball that broke through the outer wall. San Lorenzo's heaviest guns commanded the river's mouth; a rock ledge, visible only at low tide, formed an extra barrier. Lighter guns covered the drawbridge and ravine.

The buccaneers anchored in a secluded bay and marched overland, a distance of six miles. At two o'clock in the afternoon, they reached the peak opposite the main gate, only to find the drawbridge raised. Bradley lost no time in ordering an assault. His men, equally impatient, sprang into action. "Come on!" they shouted as they headed for the ravine.[15]

Don Pedro de Lisaldo, the Spanish commander, let them get as close as possible. Then the castle's walls spewed a hurricane of fire and iron. Solid shot whistled overhead or bounced off the sides of the ravine. Musket balls pinged against stones or pierced human bodies with a sickening *thud*. Men's skulls blew apart, sending bone fragments flying in all directions. Human bone is hard, and anyone hit by a piece of a comrade also fell wounded, sometimes dead. Blood made the grass slippery, causing the attackers to trip over their own feet.

It was more than flesh could bear. The buccaneers retreated, ranting and cursing. And as they left, Spaniards rose from cover to taunt them. *"Victoria, victoria, victoria,"* they chanted. "Come on, ye English dogs, enemies of God and our king! Let your other companions that are behind come on too! Ye shall not go to Panama this bout!"[16]

Bradley's men had their pride, too. After reaching the safety of the jungle, they lay down to rest until dark. Apart from a cannonball now and then, everything was quiet, and many fell asleep.

Once darkness came, however, the buccaneers came like a whirlwind.

Although the Spaniards answered as before, courage had nothing to do with what happened next. The attackers seemed about to give way again when sheer luck turned the tide of battle. A buccaneer felt an arrow plunge into his left side, below the ribs. It hurt, and took his breath away, but had not hit a fatal spot. Pulling the arrow out, he angrily tore off part of a sleeve, wrapped the cloth around the shaft, and shot it back with his musket. Exploding gunpowder set the cloth on fire.

The arrow flew over the wall, trailing a banner of flame. Moments later, it lodged in the roof of an ammunition shed thatched with palm leaves. The shed exploded, igniting its neighbors like a string of firecrackers. In this emergency, most Spaniards had to fight the blaze, leaving large sections of the wall unguarded. The buccaneers saw their chance and ran forward, throwing grenadoes as they came. Within minutes, the entire wall was aflame, too. As the flames took hold, the timbers weakened, allowing the earth to break through and slide into the ravine. Spaniards, outlined against the leaping flames, made perfect targets for Bradley's sharpshooters.

Daylight revealed a heap of smoldering charcoal where the wall had stood. Still, the battle was far from over. Fearing torture if captured, the defenders vowed to sell their lives dearly. So, when the buccaneers charged, they stood their ground with muskets, swords, and pikes.

A sleepless night of fighting fires had left the defenders exhausted. Steadily, they gave way before the onslaught. Esquemeling tells how, as the end drew near, "the Spaniards who remained alive cast themselves down from the castle into the sea," choosing death rather than surrender.[17] Only thirty survived, not one of them an officer. A Frenchman found Don Pedro de Lisaldo's body. A musket ball had blown away half his skull, but he still held his sword. The buccaneers counted thirty killed and seventy-six wounded, among them Captain Bradley, near death with both legs shattered by a cannonball. As Bradley slipped into unconsciousness, he learned that eight Spaniards had fled up the Chagres in a canoe. Their destination: the city of Panama.

Morgan's fleet arrived the following day, January 7. As the coast came into view, lookouts saw the English flag atop San Lorenzo. In their rush to be the first ashore, the crews became careless—stupidly so. Four vessels, including the *Satisfaction,* ran up on the rock ledge and held fast. It took the waves less than four hours to pound them to bits. Several crew members drowned, but most managed to get ashore in longboats.

San Lorenzo's guns fired a salute, while a greeting party carried the chief ashore on their shoulders. "Enough!" Morgan growled; they had work to do. His close call at Lake Maracaibo had taught him never to plunge into enemy territory without first securing a line of retreat. Before continuing, therefore, he ordered the castle repaired and left six hundred men to guard it and the fleet.

The distance from San Lorenzo to Panama was forty miles as the crow flies. Morgan planned to cover the first twenty-five miles by sailing up the Chagres. The river ended at Venta de la Cruz, or Inn of the Cross, a jungle village with a wayside church. From there it was only a day's march to Panama. Morgan expected to reach his objective in two days at the very most, but in fact the journey would take nine of the worst days of his life.

Morgan had arrived in the dry season, and this year the river was lower than usual. Fortunately, his men found scores of Indian canoes and thirty-six Spanish *chatas*, flat-bottomed riverboats, near the castle. Rather than overload the flimsy craft, he decided to leave the food behind, relying upon supplies captured along the way. Ordinarily, that would not have been a problem; before leaving on a raid, buccaneers never had trouble getting Spanish supplies. Moreover, Spaniards raised cattle and grew crops within a few miles of the Chagres.

This time, however, Morgan miscalculated. The reason had less to do with geography than with the man himself. By early 1671, he had fallen under the spell of his own fame and "habit" of success. The buccaneer chief had developed boundless confidence in himself. Success created a sense of invincibility, always a dangerous flaw in a leader. At the same time, in his contempt for the Spaniards, he did not believe them capable of doing the obvious: starving the invaders by burning their own property.

On January 9, Morgan set out with his motley collection of river craft. The area he passed through no longer exists as he saw it—thanks to modern technology. It has vanished beneath the waters of Lake Gatun, a vast artificial lake formed during construction of the Panama Canal. But the buccaneers' journey up the Chagres was an ordeal unlike any they had ever experienced.

The shallow river twisted in tight loops, forcing the boats to pass near places they had left behind hours earlier. Rowers wasted their energy in a series of weed-filled pools joined by shallow rapids that flowed over jagged rocks. Gnarled roots of mangrove trees broke the surface close to shore, while tangles of rotting tree trunks, washed downstream in past rainy seasons, jutted from the mud. After an exhausting day, Esquemeling writes, they spent the night "with only a pipe of tobacco, without any other refreshment."[18] And that was just the beginning.

On the second day, January 10, the buccaneers dragged their boats across sandbanks or lifted them over fallen trees. In several places, they had to land their fighting gear, carry the boats over an obstacle, and reload them on the other side—only to repeat the process time and again. This was hard, dangerous work, made worse by their fear of the lords of the Chagres: alligators. Few Europeans had ever seen these terrifying reptiles; they did not exist in the West Indies. Often growing eighteen to twenty feet in length, they lay submerged in the shallows, with only eyes and snouts exposed, waiting for a meal of tasty man-meat.

On the third morning, Morgan decided to leave the boats and strike overland on foot. That, too, was an error. The Panamanian jungle is nothing like the forests of Hispaniola or Jamaica. Buccaneers found the jungle "very dirty and irksome," yet also a place of astonishing beauty.[19] Wherever they turned, they saw passion flowers of the reddest red and pinkish-purple orchids clinging to tree trunks. Clouds of morpho butterflies, disturbed while drinking, rose on metallic blue wings from the edges of mud puddles. Giant mahogany and cedar trees soared skyward. Vines and creepers wove countless smaller trees and bushes into solid walls of foliage. The thick canopy retained heat, creating a steamy haze that made every step an ordeal.

Sweating and panting, the buccaneers plodded for long stretches up to their ankles in foul-smelling mud, or sank up to their waists in pools covered with slimy green algae. Razor-sharp thorns tore their clothes and bodies, so that the tiniest scratch stung when bathed in salty sweat. Bloodsucking leeches dropped onto their exposed skin from the tall grass. Wood ticks burrowed into their flesh, while red fire ants stung any exposed areas. Gnats and mosquitoes buzzed around their faces, invading their mouths if they tried to speak. Boa constrictors fifteen feet long and a foot around draped their bodies on overhanging branches, waiting for a meal. Monkeys swung and chattered through the treetops. Flocks of gaudy parrots cawed as they flew overhead.

By nightfall, Morgan had to admit defeat and return to the boats. Nature and hunger, not Spanish steel, had become his worst enemy.

The residents of Panama learned of the approaching danger at about this time, and the news threw them into a panic. Morgan's reputation had preceded him. In that superstitious age, overcoming "impossible" odds could mean but one of two things: God's favor, or Satan's. Clearly, Spaniards believed, God could not favor this monster in the form of a man. So, with each new exploit, Morgan grew in their eyes. In time, he became more of a legend than a human being. People did not—dared not—speak his name without crossing themselves. Instead, they saw him as *El Draque,* the demon Francis Drake risen from the grave. As their grandparents had talked of Drake in hushed tones, they called Morgan *El hijo del Diablo,* the devil's son. They accused *El negro Morgan,* Black Morgan, of performing the "Miracles of Satan." Ten feet tall, with red eyes able to burn holes in human flesh, he stank of brimstone, breathed flames from his nostrils, and shot bullets from his fingertips! Mothers warned their children that Morgan would bite off their heads if they misbehaved.

Don Juan Pérez de Guzmán had recently become Panama's governor. A devout Catholic, this veteran of the European wars organized the city's defenses. Believing that its main line of defense rested not on Earth, but in heaven, Don Juan turned to God and His saints. He ordered everyone, including slaves, to observe a day of prayer, fasting, and repentance.

Panama's churches filled to overflowing. Processions led by priests and nuns moved through the dusty streets behind banners embroidered with images of Christ crucified. Some monks dragged heavy wooden crosses and whipped themselves to make the blood flow; that way, they thought, God might forgive Panama's sins.

To show his sincerity, the governor gave away his personal fortune. From his treasure chests he gave saints' statues, gifts of gold chains encrusted with diamonds. His servants carried sacks of doubloons to churches in payment for war prayers. Nobody prayed harder or more fervently than the donor himself: "God, who watches us with the eyes of pity, give me victory over these heretical dogs."[20] As a final gesture of devotion, Don Juan promised the Virgin Mary to die before allowing heathens to set eyes on her image.

Panamanians also knew that God helps those who help themselves. Worried citizens hid their most valuable possessions. Priests threw silver candlesticks and jeweled chalices into wells, or walled them up with bricks. Sailors loaded wagons full of sacred objects aboard a galleon called *La Santissima Trinidada,* or *The Blessed Trinity*. Nobody knows the fate of Panama's greatest treasure, the golden altar of Saint Anastasius. One legend says a priest painted it to look like ordinary stone; another says the priests who buried it died in the fighting, taking their secret to the grave. Whatever the truth may be, the altar vanished. Some historians doubt that it ever existed.

Thousands fled Panama aboard ships. Still others had no

intention of abandoning homes they had lived in all their lives. These Panamanians grabbed weapons and joined the soldiers camped in the main plaza.

Don Juan meant to fight the invader before he reached Panama. The civilian volunteers, however, demanded that he concentrate his forces in the city itself. He objected, saying the walls needed repair. Yet they refused to listen. And since they far outnumbered the military, the brave soldier had to go along. Nevertheless, he sent a few untrained units into the jungle to fight delaying actions. Messengers also roused hundreds of Indians with tales of the devilish Morgan. Only these men, and hunger, stood between the buccaneer chief and his golden prize.

Acting on their own, Spanish settlers followed a "scorched earth" strategy. As Morgan's army approached, they burned their plantations and fled into the jungle with their farm animals. Still, seasoned hunters like the buccaneers should have had no difficulty finding food. Wild hogs and cattle, deer and turkey, roamed the countryside. Apart from shooting a rare monkey or bird, however, the invaders went hungry. The explanation is simple: twelve hundred men made lots of noise—so much that they scared away the game. Thus, in a land of plenty these crack shots grew hungrier. Nor did they fish in the Chagres. Nobody, it seems, had thought of bringing fishhooks or nets.

January 12. The fourth day. While the boats carried only the sick, their comrades now went entirely afoot. Desperate for any morsel of food, they gnawed on their leather belts, keeping their pantaloons up with bits of rope; others chewed grass and young leaves. A fortunate few roasted a snake or a mouse, eating it with a cocked pistol in hand. Toward noon, they came to an abandoned ambuscade; that is, a wall of tree trunks looped for muskets. The

Spaniards had fled, taking their food with them. Buccaneers declared, half in jest, they would gladly eat the fugitives, raw and without salt.

A search party found a pile of untanned leather sacks, all empty. No matter. Isn't leather simply beef in another form? Esquemeling, who shared the meal, never forgot how they prepared it:

> They made a huge banquet upon those bags of leather. . . . Some who never were out of their mothers' kitchens may ask how these [men] could eat and digest those pieces of leather, so hard and dry. Unto whom I only answer: That could they once experiment what hunger, or rather famine, is, they would certainly find the manner, by their own necessity, as the [buccaneers] did. For these first took the leather, and sliced it in pieces. Then they did beat it between two stones, and rub it, often dipping it into the water of the river to render it by these means supple and tender. Lastly, they scraped off the hair, and roasted and broiled it upon the fire. And, being thus cooked, they cut it into small morsels, and eat it, helping it down with frequent gulps of water, which by good fortune they had nigh at hand.[21]

Still they kept going, stumbling along dizzily, tortured by cramps every step of the way. They moved like sleepwalkers, unaware of their surroundings until they tripped over a root or stumbled into a comrade. Their minds wandered, and more than one fellow thought himself back at Port Royal, eating to his heart's content. Perhaps their chief tasted his wife's cooking—*if* she cooked. No account of the march to Panama mentions how Morgan got along.

Yet one thing is certain: he did not eat any more than the lowliest buccaneer.

On the sixth day, January 14, they came to a barn filled with Indian corn, or maize. Like men gone insane, they pushed handfuls of the uncooked grain into their mouths, while their bellies wrestled with the bullet-hard kernels. After swallowing all they could, they filled their hats with the leftovers and continued the march.

A few miles from the barn, they met an Indian war party. Actually, the Indians met them first—with a shower of arrows shot from ambush. Yet the Indian warriors had no intention of fighting a battle; that was not their way with enemies carrying muskets. Satisfied with killing three or four buccaneers, they fled into the jungle. As they went, they shouted in Spanish: "*Ha! perros, á la savana, á la savana!* Ha, ye dogs! go to the plain; go to the plain!"[22] They meant the Plain of Matasnillos. Given the invaders' condition, it seemed that nothing could prevent the Spaniards from wiping them out.

Dawn of the seventh day, January 15, found the buccaneers hungrier than ever. Venta de la Cruz lay just ahead. They had reached the end of the Chagres.

Smoke rose above the village. Surely it came from cooking fires, they thought. Quickening their pace, they tasted the food in their imagination. Upon reaching the village, however, their hearts sank. The place was a heap of smoking rubble with a few stray cats and dogs roaming about. These they killed at once, eating them half raw but "with great appetite"—if we are to believe Esquemeling.[23] A further search turned up a large sack full of bread and sixteen jars of Peruvian wine, each containing five gallons of the red liquid. Those nearest the prize quickly bit off a chunk of bread and gulped a mouthful of wine. Just as quickly they grabbed their stomachs. "Poison!" they screamed in agony; the "cowardly" Spaniards had poisoned them. Not so. For over a week, they had been surviving on "manifold sorts of trash."[24] The bread and wine triggered a normal reaction after days of extreme hunger. Everyone, apparently, recovered.

Next morning, they left Venta de la Cruz. The jungle gradually thinned as they climbed into the rugged hills that form the center of the isthmus. These hills are part of the Cordillera, the mountain range that stretches unbroken from Alaska to the tip of South America. Now every step was an ordeal for the starving men. Had the Spaniards attacked in force, they might easily have eliminated the buccaneer threat forever. But they did not. Apart from an occasional cavalry patrol, Panama's defenders stayed close to their city.

The trek ended dramatically. On the ninth day, January 17, Morgan led the column to the top of a hill local people still call El Cerro de los Bucaneros, The Hill of the Buccaneers. Reaching the crest, the buccaneers froze in their tracks. A marvelous new world lay at their feet. Off to the west, church spires rose in the distance. Beyond them, reaching to the far horizon, lay the blue Pacific. Six ships, led by a galleon under full sail, had just left port and could be seen heading out into the Bay of Panama. Morgan gave no hint of his feelings at this time. His men, however, could not contain their emotions. Although hungry as ever, they shouted, tossed their hats into the air, and jumped for joy.

Stumbling down the hill, they shouted even louder. There, calmly grazing in a meadow, was a herd of cattle the Spaniards had forgotten to drive away. Without realizing it, those responsible for this error—whoever they were—had signed Panama's death warrant. Real food would strengthen the buccaneers for the fight ahead.

Cutlasses and knives glinted in the sunlight. Laughing buccaneers ran among the bawling beasts, stabbing and slashing with all their might. "Thus cutting the flesh of these animals into convenient pieces," says Esquemeling, "they threw them into the fire, and, half-roasted, they devoured them with incredible haste and appetite. For such was their hunger that they more resembled cannibals than Europeans at this banquet, the blood . . . running down their beards unto the middle of their bodies."[25] Satisfied at last, they lay down to digest the meal.

Morgan let them rest during the hottest part of the day. At four in the afternoon, he ordered the march to continue. No longer were his followers a mob of starving vagabonds. They were an army.

Another two hours brought them to the Plain of Matasnillos. Ahead lay the tiled roofs and church spires of the city of Panama. Morgan decided to make camp and fight after a good night's sleep.

The Spaniards decided to give them no rest. Toward sunset, two hundred horsemen galloped into view. Halting just beyond musket range, they shouted a challenge: "*Perros! nos veremos!* Ye dogs! we shall meet ye!"[26] But instead of charging, they sped away as quickly as they had come. Moments later, cannons fired from atop the city walls, and kept firing throughout the night. The cannons, however, were too far away to do any serious harm. Solid shot bounced harmlessly in the darkness while the buccaneers snored.

January 18. A clear, sunny day. A day of battle.

After a hasty breakfast of beef, the army prepared for action.

Each man wiped the jungle's dirt from his musket and pistols. Then he unloaded each piece and fired, to remove any rust from inside the barrel. After that he reloaded, this time with lead.

Morgan snapped a command. Drums rolled. Trumpets blared. Flag bearers took their places. Twelve hundred fighting men fell into line. Another command set the entire body in motion.

The Battle of Matasnillos would prove to be Henry Morgan's masterpiece. How he learned to fight the way he did that day is a mystery. He had never commanded so many men in action, or faced so large an enemy force. Perhaps he had read up on the battles of the Thirty Years' War, or had sought advice from veterans like his uncles. One thing is certain: his plan was nothing new. It would have been familiar to any experienced European officer.

Morgan adopted the *tercio*, or "group of three," as his battle formation. Seen from above, the *tercio* resembled an elongated diamond pointed at either end. The first section faced forward, toward the enemy, a human wedge three hundred strong. Led by John Morris and Lawrence Prince, both able fighters, it was the army's vanguard, or leading edge. Behind it came the second section, or van—the main body. This consisted of two three-hundred-man units standing side by side and separated by a narrow pathway. Morgan commanded the right-hand unit, the position of honor; Edward Collier, another old buccaneer, commanded the unit to his left. The third section was an exact copy of the first, only it pointed backward to guard the army's rear and line of retreat. Its leader was Bledry Morgan, the chief's cousin and a recent arrival in the West Indies. All sections had a space of about twenty yards between them, allowing each to advance or fall back, either together or separately. The chief sent his orders by messenger or by trumpet call.

Morgan halted the advance between a low hill and a stretch of marshy ground. Ahead stood the men of Panama, blocking his way. Governor Juan Pérez de Guzmán sat on a jet black stallion, clad in a polished steel helmet with a peacock plume and a steel breastplate covered by a silk cape embroidered with golden lions. His Excellency commanded fourteen hundred foot soldiers—musketeers, pikemen, swordsmen, archers—drawn up in a line six deep. At least half were men of color: mulattoes, *zambos*, slaves. Man for man, they were no match for the invaders. Few had ever heard shots fired in anger or seen what a musket ball could do to a human body. The musketeers had outdated weapons, not buccaneering-pieces that could shoot twice as far. Two cavalry squadrons, totaling four hundred riders, stood to the right and left of the infantry line. Each rider carried a sword, two pistols, and an eight-foot lance tipped with a steel point and a colorful pennant. Don Juan's "secret weapon" grazed nearby, unseen behind a hill in the invaders' rear. It was a herd of fifteen hundred bulls guarded by Indian cowboys. Surely, he thought, a stampede at the right time would leave behind nothing but broken weapons and bloody rags.

The Spaniards were not impressed with the look of the buccaneers. Gazing across the plain, they saw not able soldiers, but ragged ruffians. And the buccaneers certainly behaved that way at first glance. Some had saved a little wine from Venta de la Cruz. Now they drank it up. One fellow broke ranks, dropped his pantaloons, and shook his bare bottom at the enemy. His comrades stood in place, waving their weapons and bawling drunken songs.

In Amsterdam there dwelt a maid,
Her cheeks was red, her eyes was brown,
Her hair like glow-worms hanging down.

Spaniards turned to each other. "We have nothing to fear," they said, grinning. "There are not more than six hundred drunkards."[27]

They were still grinning when Morgan barked another command. "Forward!"

His men began moving in perfect military formation. Such precision was not accidental; it took weeks of training to perfect this maneuver. Not all buccaneers were former sailors. Many, no doubt, had served in Cromwell's army or as mercenaries in the Thirty Years' War.

A trumpet call set the Spanish cavalry in motion.

"Santiago! Santiago y a ellos!" they shouted, calling upon Spain's patron saint for courage. "Saint James! Saint James and at them!"

First at a slow trot, then at full gallop, the squadrons swept across the plain. *"Viva el Rey!"* they shouted, swords and lances pointing toward the column ahead. "Long live the king!"

The buccaneers came to a halt. Nobody spoke. Only the fluttering of flags broke the silence. Seconds later, they saw bearded faces, red lips, and white teeth under steel helmets.

When the Spaniards drew close enough for the buccaneers to see the "whites of their eyes," the vanguard dropped to one knee, aimed, and fired. Like automatic killing machines, each rank fired while the others reloaded, keeping up a steady volley.

The effect was awesome. Riders plummeted to the ground,

bouncing and rolling until they lay still. Shot from the saddle, men fell screaming as feet got caught in stirrups, dragging them along the ground. Bellies torn open and trailing coils of gray intestines, horses plunged and reared, their eyes glazed with terror. Everywhere torn bodies of men and horses mingled in death.

Yet the Spaniards were brave men. Unwilling to accept defeat, they rallied and charged repeatedly. It was all for nothing. They withdrew after an hour, leaving most of their comrades on the field. The buccaneers rose, reloaded, and moved forward. Ahead lay the Spaniards' main force.

Don Juan had ordered the infantry not to attack without his signal. The infantry's left wing, however, included survivors of Puerto Bello. These men had scores to settle with the buccaneers. So, after the defeat of the cavalry, their anger overcame their discipline. It happened so quickly that Don Juan, commanding the right wing in person, could hardly believe his eyes. Instead of waiting for orders, the left wing broke ranks and charged. At first, it made progress. The forward momentum carried it through and around Morgan's vanguard. Moments later, it approached his main force.

Six hundred buccaneers halted, aimed, and fired at close range. Their volley exploded in the Spaniards' faces, shrouding everything in a cloud of smoke. Moments later, a breeze blew the smoke away, revealing scores of Spanish bodies and the survivors in retreat.

Defeated at every turn, Don Juan decided to risk everything in a last desperate effort. He ordered the *vaqueros* to drive their bulls around the hill behind Morgan's army, while he attacked head-on with his remaining troops.

Turning in the saddle, His Excellency raised his sword for

everyone to see. "Come along, boys!" he shouted. "There is no other remedy now but to conquer or die! Follow me!"[28]

The Spaniards charged—right into a wall of hot lead. With each step, dozens fell silently or rolled on the ground, thrashing in pain.

Enough! After fifteen minutes of butchery, they, too, fled. Their commander, however, kept moving forward, alone except for a black servant. Don Juan had vowed to defend Panama with his last breath. He would have done just that, had a priest named Juan de Dios (John of God) not seen him from the distance. Rushing to the governor's side, he said that God did not wish him to commit suicide. Don Juan turned back, believing that God had spoken through the holy man's mouth. Only "a miracle of the Virgin," he claimed in his official report, could have "brought me off safe among so many thousand bullets."[29]

Meanwhile, the cowboys started the bulls moving with whips and lance points. The frightened animals lowered their heads and stampeded.

Ordinary soldiers would have panicked at the sight of thousand-pound bulls bearing down on them with sharp horns. Yet buccaneers had seen it all before, in Hispaniola, and knew how to deal with stampedes. The rear guard calmly waited until the right moment and then, just as calmly, shot the lead animals between the eyes. The rest veered off and kept going, straight toward the oncoming Spaniards, scattering them like leaves before the wind.

That did it! "We pursued the enemy so close," Morgan reported, "that their retreat came to plain running." Thus ended the Battle of Matasnillos. In two hours of fighting, his army had killed some five hundred Spaniards at a cost to itself of five dead and ten wounded.[30]

The battle for Panama City, 1671. From the French edition of Esquemeling's *The Buccaneers of America.*

The buccaneers swept into Panama on the heels of its defenders. Facing only scattered resistance, they started breaking into wine shops and looting warehouses along the waterfront. Morgan let them "enjoy" themselves for the time being. After an hour, he sent word that the Spaniards had poisoned the wine. They had done no such thing, but he wanted them sober in case Don Juan rallied his forces.

Meanwhile, His Excellency made the most important deci-sion of his life. Rather than allow these cutthroats to ravage his beloved Panama, he had soldiers prepare it for destruction. As the conquerors busied themselves with looting, Spaniards operating in small groups placed kegs of gunpowder in houses located at key points in the city. Before fleeing into the countryside, the gov-ernor ordered the kegs detonated, together with Panama's main gunpowder magazine. A series of explosions shook the ground at five-minute intervals. "Burn, burn!" citizens cried as flames leapt skyward. "That is the order of señor Don Juan."[31]

Within minutes of the first explosion, trumpets called the buccaneers to the main plaza. From there, Morgan sent out teams of firefighters. To keep the fires from spreading, they blew up buildings in their path. Yet the fires had "long legs," as one fellow observed. Fanned by a sea breeze, sheets of flame leapt from house to house and street to street. Apart from a few buildings on the outskirts, Panama was doomed.

Morgan had no time to mourn an enemy city. He had come to Panama for treasure, and treasure he would have! At daybreak, he camped in the plaza and sent scouts into the countryside to find food. Unlike their cousins along the Chagres, plantation owners living north and south of Panama had not destroyed their crops.

To the untrained eye, it seemed that the city had nothing left to steal. Morgan knew better. True, the flames had consumed priceless fabrics and furniture. Nevertheless, much treasure remained, though in a changed form.

As the ruins cooled, search parties sifted through mounds of debris. They uncovered misshapen lumps of gold and silver, the contents of hidden money boxes melted as in an oven. From the mud at the bottom of wells evaporated by the intense heat, they took all kinds of precious things: jewelry, golden crosses, saints' statues, silverware, goblets set with emeralds and pearls.

Panama's citizens—those who had not fled—became another source of hidden treasure. Anyone who might know anything met Morgan's torturers. These men would not take no for an answer. Once they got the idea that a person was hiding something, they kept at their nasty work until the end. In one case, a rich man's

gardener had put on his master's breeches; these had a silver key hanging from a drawstring. That key cost the poor fellow his life. Esquemeling reports:

> They immediately asked him: Where was the cabinet for the said key? His answer was: *He knew not what was become of it, but only that finding those breeches in his master's house, he had made bold to wear them.* Not being able to extort any other confession out of him, they first put him upon the rack, wherewith they immediately disjointed his arms. After this, they twisted a cord about his forehead, which they wrung so hard, that his eyes appeared as big as eggs, and were ready to fall out of his skull. But neither with these torments, could

The sack of **P**anama **C**ity by **H**oward **P**yle, *Harper's Magazine,* **A**ugust and **S**eptember, 1887.

they obtain any positive answer to their demands. Where-upon they . . . [gave] him infinite blows and stripes. . . . Af-terwards they cut off his nose and ears, and singed his face with burning straw, till he could speak nor lament his misery no longer. Then losing all hopes of hearing any confession from his mouth, they commanded a negro to run him through with a lance, which put an end to his life, and a period to their cruel and inhumane tortures. After this execrable manner did many others of those miserable prisoners finish their days. . . . [The buccaneers] spared, in these their cruelties, no sex nor condition whatsoever.[32]

As we have seen, these "cruel and inhumane tortures" were usual in the seventeenth century. English and Spanish law, for example, provided for far more severe punishment for anyone found guilty of treason.

Victims swore that much of Panama's treasure was safe aboard ship; in fact, the same vessels the invaders had seen from the hilltop. A quick search turned up a small coastal craft, which the Spaniards had run aground but failed to burn. Morgan had her repaired and put under the command of Captain Robert Searle, a veteran sea rover with many prizes to his credit. Within a few days, Searle captured three other vessels. With this tiny "fleet," he visited the islands in the Bay of Panama. More often than not, he found refugees from the city. Faced with torture, or with seeing their loved ones tortured, they led Searle to their be-longings.

La Santissima Trinidada, the richest prize of all, escaped through the buccaneers' own stupidity. After landing on the is-land of Tobago, they found barrels of wine in a cellar and began to get drunk. Meanwhile, the Spanish captain, ignorant of their arrival, sent a shore party to get freshwater from a stream, only to have it captured. The sailors admitted under torture that the galleon was nearby; better yet, she had only seven cannons, the rest having gone overboard to make room for passengers and treasure. Captain Searle, more sober than the rest, wanted to go after her immediately. His men refused. Those who had not passed out were having too much fun to break up the party. The Spanish captain, however, was growing suspicious. When the shore party failed to return after a few hours, he headed south, toward the port of Quito, Ecuador. Next morning, Searle's men awoke with pounding headaches and "morning-after" tempers, made worse by the realization that they had traded a huge treasure for a drunken frolic.

It took Morgan four weeks to pick Panama clean. On February 14, 1671, he had the purchase loaded onto 175 mules. His human booty stood nearby, downcast and miserable. Four hundred of these were black slaves. Nothing could change their fate; they had merely exchanged masters. There were also two hundred white people—men, women, children—destined for sale into slavery if their relatives did not meet Morgan's ransom demands. Women fell to their knees and begged him to return them to their loved ones. The buccaneer chief closed his heart to their pleas, showing no sign of human sympathy or mercy. He had not come so far to hear whining women, he sneered, "but rather to seek moneys; therefore they ought to seek that out."[33] Then he gave the order to march, turning his back on the ruined city.

Everyone turned away. *Panama la Vieja*, Old Panama, never recovered. Returning citizens stood speechless before the charred rubble. Not only had their homes vanished, life for many could never be the same. They had lost too much, seen too much, to go on as if nothing had happened. The place held such terrible memories that they could not bring themselves to rebuild. They decided to move their city to its present location seven miles to the west. Nowadays, Old Panama is a tourist attraction. Foreigners, many of them English, wander amid the ruins, which are silent reminders of a glorious past and a violent man's greed.

Morgan reached Venta de la Cruz in less than a day. There he found his river fleet waiting to take the army down the Chagres; heavy rains had raised the water level, allowing boats to move downstream with ease. For nine days, until February 24, he "refreshed" his men, while relatives ransomed most of his white captives. Yet all was not well. Rumor had it that certain officers, including the chief, had put aside part of the treasure for themselves; next to cowardice in battle, this was the worst offense a buccaneer could commit.

Morgan decided to stop the grumbling at once. On their last morning in the village, he called a surprise meeting before breakfast. As the buccaneers gathered, his most trusted men stood nearby, their muskets at the ready. To set an example, Morgan stripped naked while a committee, chosen by the men, examined every stitch of his clothing. They found nothing, as he knew they would. He then ordered everyone searched from head to toe. Some protested, particularly the French, insulted that anyone might question their honesty. Morgan insisted, and none dared disobey; that commission in his baggage gave his words the force of law.

So, after allowing themselves to be searched, representatives of each group examined their comrades' clothes. As an added precaution, they took apart every musket to make sure nothing was hidden in the barrel, or between the stock and barrel. Only a few items turned up, yet nothing worth the hatred many now felt for their chief. The search over, they boarded the boats and floated down the Chagres, a journey lasting two days. It was a pleasure. Not once did they have to trudge along the shore or carry the boats over sandbanks.

Back at San Lorenzo, Morgan divided the spoils. The total—in gold, silver, jewels, slaves—came to 375,000 pieces of eight. Each man received two hundred pieces of eight; that is, £20 in English money or its equivalent value in slaves. Men's hearts sank. Twenty pounds! Twenty measly pounds! Blast it all! That came nowhere near the £150 share from Puerto Bello.

Something smelled fishy, buccaneers growled. They had endured so much, fought so hard—and for *this*! How could it be? The answer came in the same breath as they asked the question. Someone had cheated them. *Harry Morgan* had cheated them, damn his eyes! Angry, bitter men crowded around Morgan, cursing him to his face. He said nothing and showed no emotion except a tightness at the corners of his mouth. Escorted by a few trusted bodyguards, he walked toward his tent. His right hand rested on the hilt of a sword, his left on the silver handle of a pistol.

Morgan was capable of cheating his comrades—of cheating *anyone*. Whether he did actually cheat his men, however, is another question. More than three centuries later, we have no way of discovering the truth. We can be certain, however, that Morgan feared for his life. After so many years, after so many exploits, the old magic was gone; he had lost the buccaneers' trust forever.

During the night of March 6, Morgan secretly sailed aboard the *Mayflower* in company with three other ships. The French wanted to go after him, to blow him out of the water, but he made sure to escape with the supply ships. Those left behind had little food and could not put to sea until they found more.

While they swore and threatened, Morgan set a course for Port Royal, arriving there exactly three weeks later. The rest of the fleet separated at the mouth of the Chagres. French vessels cruised along the Mexican coast, returning to Tortuga over a period of five months. The English buccaneers eventually made their way to Port Royal. By then, however, no one cared to hear their tale of treachery. Most Jamaicans hailed Morgan as their savior.

On May 31, 1671, Sir Thomas Modyford called a special meeting of the Council of Jamaica. It had only one item on the agenda: Henry Morgan. After discussing his recent expedition, the council gave him "many thanks" for his services to Jamaica and "approved very well of his acting."[34]

Five

Into the Sunset

You was a flyer, Morgan,　　　You was a great one, Morgan,
And was the lad to crowd,　　You was a king uncrowned,
When you was in your flagship,　When you was under canvas,
But now you're in your shroud.　But now you're underground.
　　　　　　　　　　　　　　　—anonymous poem, c. 1689

Spaniards could not remember anything like it. The actions of a single person, Henry Morgan, had sent their entire country into mourning. When news of Panama's destruction reached Spain, millions of ordinary people put on black armbands and flocked to their churches. At El Escorial, the sprawling palace outside the capital, Madrid, the royal family spent hours in its private chapel, begging God to rise up in His wrath and destroy their diabolical enemy.

Losing a great city in wartime is a tragedy. Yet Spaniards could have accepted their loss, because such things happen when nations fight. Morgan, however, had struck his heaviest blow in peacetime—and that was intolerable.

Not only had Spain and England been at peace since King Charles II came to the throne in 1660, they had worked hard to strengthen the original treaty. On July 8, 1670, nine days after the

Council of Jamaica had voted to turn Morgan loose, diplomats had signed the Treaty of Madrid, one of the most important agreements in modern history. Both nations pledged to stop all raiding in the New World, cancel all privateering commissions, and forget past wrongs "as if they had never happened." Moreover, for nearly two centuries Spain had claimed that she alone owned everything west of the Line. Thanks to Morgan's earlier raids, she had abandoned that claim. In the treaty's last article, Spain recognized England's right to the islands occupied or captured in the past fifty years. Now Panama threatened to undo the achievement of Madrid.

His Majesty did not know whom to believe. Sir Thomas Modyford insisted that the attack had been a sad, though unavoidable, error. Not only had Spanish privateers forced his hand, he explained, but London had taken five months to send him a copy of the Treaty of Madrid. By the time it arrived, Morgan was at Cow Island with his fleet. On December 18, the governor sent him an order to return to Port Royal at once. It had arrived too late. Morgan had sailed ten days earlier, and there was no way of reaching him—or so Modyford said.

"*Ridículo!*" sneered the Spanish ambassador, most undiplomatically. "Ridiculous!" Count Molina insisted that Modyford had had plenty of time to cancel the raid. However, the governor never had any intention of doing so, the count said, because he and "the pirate" were partners in crime. If he had sent Morgan a pullback order, he must also have sent a secret letter urging him to leave without delay. Even if Morgan had already left, the governor had known his destination and could have sent a ship to head him off, the Spaniard argued.

Who was right? King Charles had no way of knowing for certain; nor do we. Yet it made no difference. The damage was already done, and he must think of the future. In the world of high politics, truth, even justice, might have to bend to the national interest. His Majesty desired peace with Spain more than ever. The year 1670 saw England and the Netherlands rapidly sliding toward another war, and he needed allies, or at least friendly neutrals. Therefore, it became a high priority to patch things up with Spain. That in turn required an English scapegoat.

King Charles summoned Sir Thomas Lynch, a wealthy Jamaican landowner, to a private meeting. Without wasting any words, His Majesty handed Lynch a letter embossed with the royal seal. The letter ordered him to return to Jamaica, take over as governor, and arrest Sir Thomas Modyford on suspicion of high treason. Not that the king meant to do him any harm. The idea was to give the appearance of action without really doing anything. He would have the former governor kept in prison until Spanish tempers cooled. That might take a few years, but the prisoner must be patient. Eventually, His Majesty would release him and give him another post.

Sir Thomas Lynch arrived at Port Royal in June 1671 aboard the warship *Assistance*. He took power at once, but dared not arrest his predecessor immediately. Friendly and generous, Modyford was so popular that Lynch feared a rebellion if he acted in haste. He worked quietly, deliberately, like a spider spinning its web strand by strand. His spies watched Modyford's every movement. Lynch lived as a guest in his house, eating his food and drinking his wines. Finally, on August 15, the governor arrested him during a banquet aboard the *Assistance*. When the prisoner objected to the trick, Lynch assured him that his life and property were in no danger.

Modyford had his doubts about this. However, his arrival in England three months later set his mind at ease. Guards took him to the Tower of London, a gloomy fortress-prison built five centuries earlier. Countless people had suffered and died behind its gray walls. Englishmen knew the importance of entering through the "right" gate. Those charged with treason passed through Traitors' Gate, a sure sign that they did not have long to live. Those held on less serious charges came through the main gate. That is how Modyford entered. Once inside, the warden escorted him not to a rat-infested dungeon but to a large, well-furnished room. As a privileged prisoner, his door stayed unlocked and he received visitors any time of the day or night. A servant tended to his needs. Lynch had been right: he need not fear. The whole business was merely a show staged for the benefit of Spain.

Act Two starred Henry Morgan. The buccaneer had returned from Panama a wealthy, though discontented, man. His health had never been worse. When his stomach did not ache, "the chill"—malaria—kept him shivering on the hottest days. Worse, those who once admired him now spat at the sound of his name. Veterans of Panama, Governor Lynch reported, "would take it for a great compliment to be severe with Morgan, whom they rail on horribly, for starving, cheating and deserting them."[1] Acting on orders from London, on April 4, 1672, he arrested Morgan and sent him to England under armed guard.

Morgan had first crossed the Atlantic as a vigorous youth of nineteen. He recrossed it as an ailing adult of thirty-seven. The man who had once commanded the beautiful *Oxford* returned to his homeland aboard a leaky tub called the *Welcome*. She was so unseaworthy that the navy took her out of service when she reached port.

The three-month voyage was a living nightmare. Storms lashed the frail craft for days without letup, making it impossible for Morgan to keep his food down. During many a sleepless night he sat in a chair, vomiting into a bucket. Yet these discomforts were mild compared to the cold. Morgan had grown used to the tropics, a world of blue skies, warm waters, and balmy breezes. In Jamaica, the daily average temperature is eighty degrees Fahrenheit. On the open Atlantic, however, it is at least twenty degrees lower. Pounding waves and windblown spray kept everything permanently damp, even in the cabins. If Morgan went topside, the wind cut him to the bone. Laid low by fever, his only relief came from the rum bottle; the alcohol warmed his insides and made him forget his misery while its effects lasted. When *Welcome* reached England, her captain described his passenger as "much tired" and "very sickly."[2]

His Majesty had no intention of harming England's greatest living sea rover. European rulers always kept men like Morgan in reserve—just in case. If they got caught in some shady activity, the ruler always had "plausible deniability"; that is, he claimed they were acting on their own. So, instead of sending Morgan to the Tower, King Charles allowed the ailing buccaneer to live in London at his own expense. That was not a hardship, since Morgan had brought a fortune in Spanish doubloons. He could afford the best London had to offer.

Morgan rented an apartment in a mansion overlooking the Thames River. Like the boy who had once marveled at Bristol, the man now set out to explore an even stranger city. A metropolis of nearly a million people, London had grown into the world's largest city. New streets and buildings had erased the scars left by the Great Fire. Wherever the visitor turned, he found an endless variety of things to see and hear, do and taste. Londoners gathered in special places to drink a brown brew from the Far East; they called them "coffeehouses." Countless taverns, or "public houses," not only served alcoholic drinks, but functioned as places for people of all classes to mingle. While bankers and merchants closed deals at one table, burglars and holdup men made plans at another.

During his wanderings, Morgan met Christopher, Duke of Albemarle, at age nineteen the third richest man in England and Sir Thomas Modyford's cousin. His Grace introduced his new friend to London's "best" people. Morgan became an instant celebrity. High society showered him with attention. There seemed no end to the banquets and balls and toasts to his health. Noblemen and their ladies gathered around to ooh and ah at his stories of adventure on the Spanish Main. In brilliant word pictures, he showed them nuns carrying ladders to the castle wall at Puerto Bello, made them experience the starving time on the isthmus, and put them in front of the bulls at Matasnillos. The buccaneer enjoyed his fame well enough. Yet even fame can become boring. Meanwhile, he waited.

King Charles was in no hurry to decide his case. Count Molina raged and threatened, but His Majesty kept putting the Spaniard off with excuses. At last, he promised to bring Morgan to trial, but only after the royal council collected every scrap of evidence in the case. Yet the council was in no hurry, either. Month after month, it gathered reports on Morgan's activities in the West Indies and along the Spanish Main. It also asked for "characters," letters from people who had known the buccaneer at various times in his life. Nobody, it seems, could find anything bad to say about him. One letter came from William Morgan, a distant cousin, who said he had "a very good character." A retired general described him as "a very well deserving person and one of great courage and conduct."[3] The council sent its information to the royal palace.

In November 1673, soldiers took Morgan to the council chamber in Saint James's Palace. There, seated at the head of a long table, he saw a tall, bony man of forty-three with a big red nose and bright blue eyes. Nicknamed the "Merry Monarch," Charles II loved power, money, and beautiful women—in that order. Where these were involved, he would never allow questions of principle to stand in the way. His Majesty may have read the council's reports. Whether he did or not, they did not influence his decision. Fact: He needed men like Morgan and would not easily part with his services. Fact: Spain was already turning its attention to fresh troubles in Europe. Morgan's trial, therefore, would simply be the final scene in a royal play.

Count Molina opened with a blistering attack on the buccaneer. The accused sat calmly, as if the charges had nothing to do with him. No reason to worry, he thought; he had an airtight defense.

When the ambassador finished, Morgan rose to tell his side of the story. That was easy enough. All he did was quote the order in his commission to "do all manner of exploits" against the enemy. *All manner of exploits!* That phrase was as broad as the Atlantic Ocean. It covered everything that happened during the raid on Panama. Nobody questioned the legality of the document, just as nobody could prove that he knew about Governor Modyford's pullback letter. End of statement. Case closed.

His Majesty leaned back in his chair, smiling. Verdict: Not guilty. England hailed the king's wisdom in the trial of her "second Drake."

There *was* a similarity between Francis Drake and Henry Morgan. Both were self-made men, having risen from humble beginnings to fame and fortune by plundering Spanish towns. Just as Queen Elizabeth I had ignored demands for Drake's execution, King Charles II acquitted Morgan. More than that, both rulers also honored their seagoing thieves. The queen dubbed Drake a knight aboard his ship, the *Golden Hind*, upon his return with a vast treasure seized along the Pacific coast of South America. The king showed his appreciation, too. A few weeks after the trial, Morgan received a solid-gold snuffbox with His Majesty's portrait set in diamonds. On January 23, 1674, he named Morgan lieutenant governor of Jamaica and knighted him in a public ceremony.

Sir Henry Morgan, Knight, spent the rest of 1674 enjoying London and advising the government on Jamaica's defense needs. Early the following year, he sailed home aboard *The Jamaica Merchant*, a splendid vessel worthy of a returning hero.[4]

Between 1675 and 1683, Sir Henry served under three governors. Several months—once even two years—elapsed between the end of one governor's term and the arrival of a replacement, leaving him as acting governor. Now the energy and creativity that had brought him fame as a buccaneer found other outlets. During those times he was acting governor, he improved the island's defenses by organizing the volunteer militia and building forts at key points along the Palisadoes; Fort Morgan, for example, had sixteen heavy cannons. Success brought other appointments: membership on the Council of Jamaica; command of the militia; the chief judgeship of the Admiralty Court. This court tried all cases relating to the law of the sea, including piracy. Governors came and went, but the lieutenant governor remained. He had become the most powerful man in Jamaica.

Yet this was not the island he had known as a young man. Sir Henry and his buccaneers had succeeded only too well. In protecting Jamaica and nourishing its economy with Spanish booty, they enabled it to prosper as never before. As a result, the old Jamaica was vanishing before their very eyes.

Sir Henry saw signs of change everywhere. By the late 1670s, Port Royal would be the busiest seaport in the New World. Its population grew from 3,500 in 1661 to over 20,000 in 1675. The town had over one thousand well-built houses, many of them three stories high. Ships arrived weekly from England, New England, Virginia, and continental Europe. These brought cargoes of building materials—bricks, shingles, tar, nails, glass—farm animals, tools, flour, guns, butter, cheese, liquor, and clothing. In return, dockworkers filled their holds with tropical products: indigo, cocoa, pineapples, oranges, tangerines, "white wool" (cotton), and sugar, the island's chief cash crop.

White Jamaicans enjoyed a standard of living most Europeans would have envied. A traveler wrote:

The heat makes many clothes intolerable, and therefore the men generally wear only thread stockings, linen drawers, and vest, a handkerchief tied around their head, and a hat above. Wigs are never used but on Sundays, or in court time; and then gentlemen appear very gay in silk coats and vests trimmed with silver. The servants wear a coarse *Osnabrig* [German linen] frock, with buttons at the neck and hands, long trousers of the same, a speckled shirt and no stockings. . . . The ladies are as gay as anywhere in Europe, dress as richly, and appear with as good a grace. . . . Negroes go mostly naked, except those who attend gentlemen, who take care to have them dressed in their own livery [family colors]. . . . The negro women go many of them quite naked . . . and are surprised at an European's bashfulness, who perhaps turns his head aside at the sight. Their masters give them a kind of petticoat, but they do not care to wear it. In the towns they are obliged to do it, and some of them there go neat enough; but these are the favorites of young squires [gentlemen], who keep them for a certain use.[5]

Without black people, white people could not have prospered. During Sir Henry's time as lieutenant governor, Port Royal replaced Panama as the slave capital of the New World. Between 1674 and 1687, slightly fewer than twenty-two thousand Africans landed from ships anchored in its harbor. The slave trade became so lucrative that King Charles gave, for a price, the Company of Royal Adventurers Trading in Africa a monopoly in carrying "black ivory" across the Atlantic. The Spanish government, eager to share in the profits, licensed Port Royal merchants to sell slaves in its colonies and taxed every sale. Everyone gained—except the victims.

Although it differed in certain details, slavery in Jamaica was like slavery throughout England's North American colonies and, later, in the United States. All slaves were equal in their bondage: they were chattels, property to be bought and sold for the benefit of others.

Slaves had no rights, even that of choosing a mate. John Taylor, an English clergyman, noted that each owner "gives to each man a wife," who must accept his choice or suffer the consequences.[6] The law also allowed masters to abuse "their" women sexually; that is, "keep them for a certain use." Masters often had children with their human "property," and the number of mulattoes born in Jamaica each year far exceeded that of white infants. In 1833, Parliament passed an Emancipation Act abolishing slavery in the British colonies. By then, however, black people had become the majority in Jamaica, far outnumbering the whites.

In Morgan's day, blacks worked as carpenters, bricklayers, stonemasons, blacksmiths, fishermen, tailors, and house servants. Scores of young black men became "wrackers," treasure hunters who dove into the holds of sunken ships equipped only with courage, determination, and an ability to hold their breath longer than anyone else. Most blacks, however, lived on sugar plantations. Black field hands plowed the soil, planted the crop, and cut the cane with machetes. Black laborers ran the crushing mills and boiling houses, turning the raw cane into cakes of sugar.

Driven by white overseers, plantation slaves started work two hours before daybreak and ended after sunset. Everybody worked, including mothers who had recently given birth. A doctor described how "when slave mothers go to work they tie the young children upon their backs. While they work they frequently give children the breast across the armpits, and let them suckle."[7] Babies suffered in the hot sun, and some died of sunstroke.

Unlike free laborers, slaves could be punished for anything, or nothing, according to their master's whims. Besides the punishment of choice, whipping, they suffered every form of torment imaginable. Take, for example, the penalty for trying to escape. In such cases, the slave had an iron collar placed around his neck with a chain attached. Then he had to bend a leg backward at the

knee, while the end of the chain was clamped to his foot. A crutch enabled him to hobble around in this painful position until he learned his lesson. If he tried to escape again, the master ordered the leg cut off at the knee.

Blacks resisted slavery in countless ways. They "accidentally" broke tools and slowed down on the job, feigning sickness or stupidity. Daring men and women escaped into the Blue Mountains, where they formed communities that lived by farming and banditry. Occasionally, as we have seen, black men joined the buccaneers. Blacks also rebelled and killed their masters. In one case, five hundred rebels stole muskets and terrorized the countryside for several weeks before their capture by the militia. White vengeance was as swift and brutal as anything the buccaneers had done to the Spaniards, or the Spaniards to the

Indians. Jean Baptiste Labat, a Catholic priest who visited Jamaica in the 1690s, portrayed slavery and cruelty as different sides of the same coin:

> The least disobedience is punished severely, and still more so are the slave risings. Despite these punishments, however, these risings occur frequently, for the poor wretches, pushed to extremes more often by their drunken, ignorant, and cruel overseers than by their masters, at last lose patience. They will then throw themselves on the man who has ill-used them and tear him to pieces, and although they are certain to receive terrible punishment they rejoice that they took vengeance on these pitiless brutes. On these occasions the English take up arms and there are massacres. The slaves who are captured are sent to prison and condemned to be passed through a cane mill [that is, crushed], or be burnt alive, or be put into iron cages that prevent any movement and in which they are hung up to branches of trees and left to die of hunger and despair. The English call this torture "Putting a man to dry."
>
> I admit that these tortures are cruel, but one should be careful before blaming the inhabitants of an island, no matter what nationality they may be, for being frequently compelled to pass the bounds of moderation in the punishment of their slaves. For it must be remembered that the object of these punishments is to make the slaves fear and respect their masters, who would otherwise become the victims of their fury. Further that the slaves usually number two to one white man and are always ready to revolt, to risk all and to commit the most horrible crimes to gain their freedom.[8]

· · ·

We have no record of Sir Henry Morgan's dealings with his own slaves, or whether they ever rebelled. All we know is that he owned 109 black people. A few, no doubt, spoke Spanish and had once walked the streets of Maracaibo and *Panama la Vieja*. Enemies accused him of many things, but never of having affairs with black women or cheating on his wife. Slavery, for him, was merely a business arrangement, a matter of profit and loss. If called upon to defend slavery, he would probably have answered like most of his white contemporaries. Hideous though their attitude was, seventeenth-century Europeans believed that Africans were closely related to apes, and thus inferior to their "natural" masters, the whites. This view of Africans helped justify the cruel and inhuman treatment characteristic of slavery and the slave trade.

Yet not all Jamaican slaves were black people. The buccaneers, as we have seen, enslaved Spaniards unable to pay their ransom. In addition, shiploads of enslaved Indians came from New England, particularly the Massachusetts Bay Colony. The God-fearing Puritans were ruthless fighters. God, they believed, had given His "saints" America as a holy land where they might worship in the "proper" manner. Well-meaning Spaniards sought to convert native peoples to Christianity, frequently by force. Frugal Puritans, however, slaughtered villages full of "red heathens" in God's name and sold the survivors into bondage in the West Indies.

Jamaica's future lay with the slaves and their masters, not Morgan's bloodthirsty crew. Privateering was an ideal start-up activity, since it required a small outlay of cash and offered quick returns. Still, in the end, it made no economic sense. The "sweet trade" discouraged lawful trade and investment in legitimate businesses. Just as lumbermen must be careful not to overcut a forest, sea rovers cannot steal too much if their victims are to survive to be plundered in the future. The sea rovers stole too much from the Spanish colonies. Although raiders would continue to strike the colonies for years to come, by the 1670s their glory days were behind them. No Jamaican would ever repeat Morgan's exploits.

Sir Thomas Lynch brought the king's order to crack down on privateering. He began by offering a pardon to any privateer for any act committed during the previous ten years. In addition, he allowed former privateers to keep their booty with no questions asked. After waiting a few weeks, he withdrew all letters of marque and reprisal. In future, he declared, these would be issued only in wartime, and only to those of "good character." To those men who left "their naughty way of life," he offered thirty-five acres of land or a cash bonus for joining the Royal Navy. Finally, the navy sent swift coast guard vessels to deal with outlaws.[9]

Nearly three hundred men accepted the governor's offer and settled down. Hundreds more returned to hunting and making *boucan* in Hispaniola. The majority, however, found that peace, like war, can be an ordeal. As with some veterans of modern wars, the way of life learned during years of fighting could not be unlearned just because governments' attitudes changed. The sweet trade was in their blood, part of their nature as human beings. With all its dangers and hardships, it drew them like an addictive drug. Where they found danger, they also found adventure; hardship also meant comradeship and good times. Abandon these? Never! With Port Royal closed to them, English buccaneers headed for Tortuga. Unlike Sir Thomas Lynch, Tortuga's French governors gladly sold privateering commissions.

Lynch's aide did not give up his old ways immediately. Although Morgan never went to sea again, he kept active behind the scenes. The former buccaneer used his official position to gather secret information, which he then sold to trusted captains. On several occasions, he sent them warnings about patrol craft and revealed the courses of Spanish galleons. At least one privateer owed his life to the lieutenant governor. Captain John Deane had been arrested for piracy and sentenced to death. Not only did Morgan halt the execution, he helped the culprit escape.

Sir Henry also encouraged English captains to go to Tortuga. Although French commissions were invalid in Jamaica, they lent a cloak of legality, however thin, to sea rovers. This practice enabled an Englishman, John Coxon, to make a fortune. In 1678, Coxon raided towns along the coast of Central America from Costa Rica to Guatemala. He then sailed to Port Royal, where Morgan allowed him to buy supplies and go on to Rhode Island to dispose of his booty. Coxon and another privateer, Richard Sawkins, later crossed the Isthmus of Panama with two hundred men, seized Spanish vessels, and cruised along the Pacific coast for eighteen months, capturing ships and looting towns. Yet New Panama was no pushover. With a garrison four times that of *Panama la Vieja*, it easily drove off the privateers. They became the first English tourists to visit the old city. "Nothing now remains of it," one wrote, "besides rubbish and a few houses of poor people." Within a decade, even these people moved away.[10]

The year 1680 marked a turning point for Morgan and the buccaneers. In May, England and Spain formally became allies. A treaty signed at Windsor Castle outside London declared that an attack by forces of any European country upon the ships or colonies of an ally meant war in Europe as well. Thus, with the stroke of a pen, the Line vanished forever. Two worlds became one. No longer might nations enjoy peace at home while fighting

across the sea. Peace became indivisible. It must reign everywhere, or nowhere.

Jamaica welcomed the treaty. In obedience to its terms, the
colonial Assembly, or legislature, passed a sweeping law. The law
made it a hanging offense for residents or vis-
itors to sail under foreign privateering commissions. France and the Netherlands soon
passed similar laws.

All this looked fine on paper. Things
turned out differently in the real world, however. Without intending it, the diplomats had
shaken a hornet's nest. For the first time in
history, thousands of experienced sea fighters stood outside the law as a group. No
longer licensed to attack Spanish shipping,
and unable to leave the sweet trade, privateers lowered their national flags and hoisted
the Jolly Roger. Except for the fact that pirates attacked ships of any nation, including
their own, there was no difference between

them and the buccaneers. Like the original buccaneers, pirates
lived as equals. A pirate vessel was a floating democracy where
crews elected their captains, signed articles, and allowed extra
shares for wounds and bravery.

Known as "Blackbeard,"
Edward Teach scoured
the coast of the Carolinas
in the early 1700s. A
fearsome character, he
always went into battle
armed to the teeth.

Pirates looked beyond Port Royal and Tortuga. The
Caribbean had yet to be completely mapped, and you could sail
for a week without sighting another vessel. There were still
dozens of uncharted cays in the Greater Antilles, fine places to
rest a crew and careen a ship. The Caribbean coasts of Honduras
and Nicaragua had scores of secluded inlets and bays from which

a small vessel could strike the unwary. There were also the Bahamas, a thinly settled chain of islands that commanded the exits from the Caribbean into the Atlantic. In less than fifty years, the buccaneers went from being peaceful hunters to fierce sea rovers and privateers. Now they embarked on the final adventure. The "golden age" of piracy had dawned. It would last in the New World for another century under leaders like William Kidd, "Long Ben" Avery, and Edward Teach, otherwise known as Blackbeard.

Sir Henry Morgan had never been sentimental about privateering. For him, the sweet trade was a means to an end, not a way of life. Although willing to risk his neck for big profits, he intended to enjoy them in peace. When privateering no longer served his purpose, he quit without ever looking back. Now a nobleman and a member of the ruling class, he became a living example of the proverb: "Set a thief to catch a thief." After the signing of the Treaty of Windsor, Sir Henry vowed to cleanse the seas of "this dangerous pestilence," as he called his former comrades.[11]

They did not leave easily. By the 1680s, English colonies had spread along the Atlantic coast of North America from Massachusetts to the Carolinas. History repeated itself. Like the Spanish colonies, these existed not for the sake of their own people, but to enrich the mother country. Parliament passed a series of Navigation Acts that allowed only English merchants to sell certain manufactured goods in the colonies, forbidding Americans to produce them on their own. The Navigation Acts later became a major cause of the American Revolution.

Colonists ignored orders against dealing with pirates. Of course they objected to piracy near their coasts; it hurt trade and raised insurance costs. Yet they saw nothing wrong with receiving goods "purchased" on the high seas. Smuggling by pirates provided needed goods at low prices. The large coastal cities—New York, Boston, Newport, Charleston—welcomed these shady characters with open arms. Colonial merchants grew wealthy without soiling their hands or drawing blood. For their part, pirates knew that if they behaved themselves in port, they could roam about freely, buy supplies, and dispose of their loot with no questions asked. His Majesty's governors realized that stamping out piracy was like bailing out a sinking ship with a teaspoon.

Sir Henry Morgan failed to stamp it out, too, but not for lack of effort. In his two years (1680–1682) as acting governor, he closed Port Royal to all ships suspected of piracy. Woe to anyone who defied the ban! Pirates unlucky enough to fall into his hands could expect no mercy. Port Royalers said, half-jokingly, that Sir Henry sent lawbreakers "up a long ladder and down a short rope." On account of Morgan, the gallows at Gallows Point, a height overlooking the harbor, seldom lacked occupants.

In June 1681, for example, a Dutchman named Jacob Everson anchored off Port Royal with a sloop he had recently captured. One night, toward midnight, Sir Henry sent a ship to seize Everson and his crew of twenty-five, the majority Englishmen. Without further ado, he turned them over to the Spaniards for execution. If he did nothing else, this proved that the old buccaneer had cut his ties to the past. "When any of the pirates are brought to me," he wrote His Majesty's council in London, "I use the utmost severity of the law against them." Not that Morgan had suddenly reformed. If he upheld the law, it was not out of respect for the law itself, but because it suited his own purposes. As the saying goes, he knew which side his bread was buttered on. He knew that now he had everything to gain by obeying the law, and every-thing to lose by breaking it.

Another time, the acting governor killed pirates with kind-ness. A mysterious vessel had anchored in Montego Bay at the western end of the island. Coast guard craft reported that her crew was behaving well enough. However, they did not go ashore, as sailors loved to do after a long voyage, but kept to themselves aboard their vessel. Back at Port Royal, Sir Henry grew suspi-cious. Something about them seemed fishy. Could they be pirates waiting for a rich prize? In their place, he would act the same way: appear harmless and strike when least expected.

Sir Henry sent the captain and his sixteen-man crew an invi-tation to dine with him at Port Royal. The invitation no longer ex-ists, but, judging from their response, it must have been quite flattering. We can imagine the crew, all Englishmen, grinning from ear to ear. Dinner with Harry Morgan! Great Morgan! Gadzooks, what an honor! Bursting with pride, they put on their best clothes and hurried to King's House, the governor's official residence.

Their host turned on the charm. Polite yet friendly, he gave a feast the likes of which these simple men could only have imag-ined until then. No *boucan* here! Uniformed slaves served one delicious course after another: roast beef, lobster, red snapper, grouper, bread and butter, fruit pie, and all the rum they could drink. The fiery brew gave them a warm glow, a sense of total well-being. It also loosened their tongues. Led on by their host's flattery, they revealed their secrets. Yes, they were pirates, with many prizes to their credit. And, yes, they were waiting in Mon-tego Bay for a merchantman to pass. Neat trick, eh? Sir Henry smiled. They kept talking, never feeling the invisible nooses slip-ping around their necks.

When they became too drunk to see straight, slaves took off their clothes and put them to bed. Next morning, the slaves woke them, served them a hearty breakfast, and bowed them out the front door. It was their last moment of freedom on the last day of their lives. No sooner did they step into the street, squinting in the sunlight, when soldiers clapped them in irons. Hustled into the Admiralty Court, they saw their host sitting in the judge's chair. No longer polite and friendly, he was cold and harsh. Before they could catch their breath, he passed sentence and begged God to have mercy on their souls. By sundown, seventeen bodies were swinging at Gallows Point.

"I abhor bloodshed," Sir Henry wrote in March 1682, "and I am greatly dissatisfied that in my short Government I have been so often compelled to punish criminals with death."[13] For those who called him a traitor to the Brethren, he had only kind words: "God forgive 'em. I do." One wonders if he meant it, or if he was having a private joke at others' expense.[14]

Sir Henry had grown used to having his own way, to acting as a law unto himself. That is a dangerous combination. Those who set themselves above the law can easily make mistakes that lead to their downfall.

His downfall began in the summer of 1683, triggered by the notorious "Mingham affair." Captain Francis Mingham aroused strong feelings in everyone he met; you either loved him or hated him. The lieutenant governor despised him, as did a certain Captain Churchill.

One morning, on Thames Street, Mingham insulted Churchill. Rather than strike back at once, that afternoon Churchill kidnapped Mingham's first mate and hoisted him naked from his ship's rigging. When Mingham protested, Churchill further gave the mate twenty lashes and tossed him into Port Royal harbor. The fellow drowned.

Mingham's friends demanded "justice." Yet, before there could be a trial, a grand jury had to decide whether a crime had actually been committed. At that point, Lieutenant Governor Morgan pressured jury members into voting that the mate had died of natural causes. Mingham cried foul, and his friends went on a rampage. For two days they broke windows, shot pistols into houses, and cracked opponents' skulls. Supporters of Sir Henry and Churchill answered in kind. Law-abiding citizens cowered behind locked doors, not daring to venture into the streets.

His Majesty had recently appointed Sir Thomas Lynch to a second term as governor. Over the years, Lynch had come to despise the lieutenant governor. Sir Henry, he felt, was a thief and a bully lacking in self-control. When drunk, he became abusive, insulting everything and everyone. "In his drink," the governor wrote, "Sir Henry reflects on the government, swears, damns and curses most extravagantly."[15] If he executed pirates, it was to make himself look good, not out of principle or for the public welfare.

The Mingham affair gave Sir Thomas an excuse to move against his aide. He built his case carefully. Throughout the summer, his agents interviewed scores of Port Royalers. They wanted to know everything about the former buccaneer. Had he ever tampered with a jury? Any dealings with pirates? Who? When? How? How much? No doubt some of their "information" was gossip, or came from those who carried a grudge. Nevertheless, other stories were undoubtedly true. A certain Mrs. Wellin, for example, testified to hearing Sir Henry shout "God damn the Assembly" as he and some drunken men passed her tavern one night. That was the last straw.[16]

On October 12, Lynch commanded Morgan to appear at a

special meeting of the Council of Jamaica. Once, the Council had relied upon him to save Jamaica from Spain. But that was long ago, and times had changed. The governor accused Morgan to his face of bribery, supporting piracy, sharing in the profits of piracy, and insulting the Assembly. In closing, he asked whether "the peace and safety of the island" required Sir Henry's dismissal. The Council's minutes record Morgan's lame reply: "he hoped he should not be charged with others' faults."[17]

Nobody *had* charged him with others' faults, only with his own misdeeds. The majority voted to expel Morgan from the Council and take away his public offices. On Lynch's recommendation, the king removed him as lieutenant governor. No one, however, could take away his knighthood. That, and his possessions, were all that remained of Morgan's glory days.[18]

Having invested heavily in land and slaves, Sir Henry was still an extremely wealthy man. At the time of his dismissal, he owned six thousand acres of land, an estate most English noblemen would have envied. Besides plantations and their buildings, his holdings included forests, fields, meadows, and streams.

Sir Henry and Lady Elizabeth Morgan lived in a two-story "great house," as West Indian planters called their homes. Their house no longer exists, but it must have followed the standard pattern. Planters' homes were miniature fortresses. Fearing slave revolts, whenever possible owners built on high ground surrounded by a clearing wider than the range of any musket. Houses had thick stone walls and shuttered windows made of a scarce timber called "bullet-wood."

The record is silent on Lady Morgan's activities. She had three sisters living in Jamaica, all married and with children; that is certain. We can imagine the childless woman visiting their homes and fussing over her nieces and nephews. Like other plantation wives, she must also have spent endless hours supervising the household slaves and keeping the accounts.

Meanwhile, her husband socialized with his neighbors. Two or three times a week, they met at someone's house to talk, eat, and drink—mostly drink. Father Biët, a visiting French priest, described a gathering of the type Sir Henry loved:

When they dine, no one is forced to drink, one drinks willingly. They present whatever drink one wants: wine from Spain, Madeira, the Canaries; French wines, and sweetened mobby [rum mixed with fruit juices] for those who do not want wine. But after one has dined, and the table has been cleared, a trencher full of pipes and another full of tobacco is put on the table along with a bowl full of brandy, into which is put plenty of sugar. . . . Egg yolks are also thrown in, then this is set alight, and they let it burn down to two-thirds of its former volume. The host takes a little silver cup, fills it with this punch and drinks to the health of whoever is in front of him. After he has drunk, he refills the cup and gives it to the person whose health he has just drunk; this person does the same thing to another, and this procedure is continued until there is nothing left in the bowl. During this festivity, well-built young slaves refill the pipes, which they present on their knees. The afternoon passes thus, in drinking and smoking, but quite often one is so drunk that he cannot return home. Our gentlemen found this life extremely pleasant.[19]

Alcohol helped Sir Henry forget. He missed power, missed having people bow low and address him as a great man. Oh, if only he could return to the Council! That would make him the happiest man alive.

In December 1687, the Duke of Albemarle arrived aboard the warship *Assistance*. Jamaica had a new governor. Suddenly, as if by a miracle, Sir Henry's fortunes seemed to revive.

Everyone who was anyone in Port Royal turned out to welcome the duke. As His Grace strode down the ship's gangplank, Morgan stepped from the crowd and extended his hand. They had not seen each other in twelve years. A person's appearance changes over time; that is natural. Seeing his friend, however, shocked the younger man. He could scarcely recognize him as the proud buccaneer he had known in London. Sir Henry was in his fifty-third year, a ripe age back then, and he showed every day of it.

Sir Hans Sloane, the duke's personal doctor, also came ashore that day. Sloane observed Morgan closely, describing him in his notes as "lean, sallow-colored, his eyes a little yellowish . . . [a man] much given to drinking and sitting up late." Experience told him that Morgan was desperately ill.[20]

The duke wrote the Royal Council on his friend's behalf. Council members acted as if they had plenty of time to reach a decision. Meanwhile, Sir Henry's time was running out—and he knew it.

On June 18, he made a will leaving his entire estate to "my very well and entirely beloved wife." Several small bequests went to his few remaining friends. These included a Spanish-style saddle, two silver-handled pistols, a silver-handled sword, and several horses. In addition, he left Morgan Byndloss, a nephew named in his honor, "ten able working negroes and two mules or two horses."[21] In the eyes of the law, black people and farm animals were the same: property to be disposed of at their owner's pleasure. In the West Indies, and later in the United States, owners left slaves in wills, gave them as wedding presents, and used them to pay debts.

In July 1688, word came that King James II had restored Morgan to the Council. By then, however, he had scarcely a month to live.[22]

Sir Hans Sloane tried to help. He ordered Morgan to stop drinking and get proper rest. The doctor also advised him to empty his stomach often, by "easy vomits with the help of a feather," and prescribed drugs such as "Oil of Scorpion."

Sir Henry was a difficult patient. He tried to follow the doctor's advice, but habit always proved stronger than willpower. By then, no doubt, he had become a confirmed alcoholic. Unable to control his craving for liquor, he drank enough to harm a person half his age. "Not being able to abstain from company," Sir Hans noted, "he sat up late drinking too much . . . [and] complained he could not make water [urinate] freely. His water was thick and very red . . . and his legs swelled a little." Day by day, Morgan's condition worsened. Eventually, "his belly swelled so as not to be contained in his coat." In addition, he coughed up blood, and hiccoughed and belched almost without letup.[23]

Sir Hans was the best physician in Jamaica, but not good enough to suit his patient. Misery drove Morgan to other men. These included a slave doctor who favored African tribal remedies. According to Sir Hans, this man gave Morgan "clysters [enemas] of urine & plastered him all over with clay and water and by it augmented his cough."[24] When these did not help, Henry sought help elsewhere, always with the same result.

He had reached the end of the line. On Saturday, August 25, 1688, at eleven o'clock in the morning, Sir Henry Morgan, the terror of the Spanish Main, died peacefully in bed. Later that day, the Duke of Albemarle ordered a state funeral.

Sunday, August 26, arrived in typical Jamaican style, with

bright sunlight and gentle sea breezes rustling the palm trees. That day, however, every fort and ship in Port Royal harbor fired a farewell salute. The funeral procession left from King's House at the stroke of noon. Everyone turned out to see a gun carriage carry Sir Henry's lead-lined coffin through the streets; His Grace had declared an amnesty, allowing even pirates to watch without fear of arrest.

Halting outside St. Peter's Church, mourners stood bareheaded while Rev. John Longworth, a buccaneer-turned-parson, read a sermon. Any historian would be glad to learn its contents, but the paper has never been found. After the service, the procession continued to a cemetery on the Palisadoes. After a few final words, workers filled up the grave and the mourners left.

Sir Henry Morgan lay under the hot sand for four years. Then, on Tuesday, June 7, 1692, nature unleashed a calamity unlike any ever seen by Europeans in the New World. For years afterward, religious people called it God's judgment on a wicked island.

June 7, 1692, was an exceptionally hot day. The sun glared in a cloudless sky, and the sea lay smooth as a mirror. At 11:40 A.M. sharp, Mr. John White took a seat next to Dr. Emmanuel Heath. As they reached for drinks, they felt a slight trembling in the ground beneath their feet. "Lord, Sir, what is that?" asked the doctor, a newcomer to Jamaica. "It is an earthquake," Mr. White replied with a wave of a hand. "Be not afraid, it will soon be over." Port Royal often had earth tremors, but they always passed without doing serious damage.[25]

Not this time. A second, more severe, shock broke the stillness with a loud *CRAAACK*. Buildings shook, and clouds of dust rose from the streets. The bell in St. Peter's steeple clanged all by itself.

The third shock split Port Royal open in a dozen places, dropping most of it into the sea. Huge tidal waves rolled over Fort Morgan, tearing ships from their anchor cables and hurling them far inland. A wave carried a French vessel into the remains of the town, only to set it down safely in the marketplace. Dr. Heath described the horrific scene in a pamphlet printed in London shortly afterward:

> The sand in the street rose like waves in the sea, lifting up all persons that stood upon it, and immediately dropping down into pits; and at the same instant a flood of water rushed in, throwing down all who were in its way; some were seen catching hold of beams and rafters of houses, others were found in the sand that appeared when the water . . . drained away, with their legs and arms out. . . . Whole streets were swallowed up by the opening earth, and the houses and inhabitants went down together. Some of them were driven up again by the sea, which arose in those breaches and wonderfully escaped. Some were swallowed up to the neck, and then the earth shut upon them, and squeezed them to death; and in that manner several were left with their heads above ground, only some heads the dogs have eaten. . . .[26]

More than two thousand people died in the earthquake itself. Disease and starvation claimed another four thousand during the following weeks. Hundreds of others met death at the hands of vengeful slaves.

The earthquake reduced the "Wickedest City in the World" to a mere ten acres of dry land. Tidal waves also destroyed the cemetery on the Palisadoes and covered miles of sea with floating

A True and Perfect Relation of that most Sad and Terrible

EARTHQUAKE, at Port-Royal in JAMAICA,

Which happened on *Tuesday* the 7th. of *June*, 1692.

Where, in Two Minutes time the Town was Sunk under Ground, and Two Thousand Souls Perished : With the manner of it at Large; in a Letter from thence. Written by Captain *Crocket* : As also of the Earthquake which happen'd in *England, Holland, Flanders, France, Germany, Ireland*, &c. And in most Parts of *Europe* : On *Thursday* the 8th of *September*. Being a Dreadful Warning to the Sleepy World: Or, God's heavy Judgments shewed on a Sinful People, as a Fore-runner of the Terrible Day of the Lord.

The EXPLANATION.

A. *The Houses Falling.* B. *The Churches.* C. *The Sugar-Works.* D. *The Mills.* E. *The Bridges in the whole Country.* F. *The Rock and Mountains.* G. *Captain Ruden's House Sunk first into the Earth, with his Wife, and Family.* H. *The Ground rolling under the Minister's Feet.* I. *The great Church and Tower falling.* K. *The Earth Opening and Swallowing Multitudes of People in Morgan's Fort.* L. *The Minister Kneeling down to a Rock with the People on the Street at Prayers.* M. *The Wharf covered with the Sea.* N. *Dr. Heath going from Ship to Ship to Visit the bruised People, and do his last Office to the dead Corpses that lay Floating from the Point.* O. *Thieves Robbing and Breaking open both Dwelling Houses and Ware-Houses during the Earthquake.* P. *Dr. Trapham, a Doctor of Physick, hanging by the Hands on a Rack of the Chimney, and one of his Children hanging about his Neck seeing his Wife and the rest of his Children a Sinking.* Q. *A Boat coming to save them.* R. *The Minister Preaching in a Tent to the People.* S. *The dead Bodies of some Hundreds floating about the Harbour.* T. *The Dead Mens Heads.* X. *Several Ships Cast away and driven into the very Town.* Y. *A Woman and her two Daughters bear to pieces one against the other.* Z. *Mr. Bockford his Digging out of the Ground.*

Port-Royal, *in Jamaica, June 30. 1792.* | Rack of a Chimney, and one of his Children hanging about his Neck, were both | Captain *Willift* and his Son, Mrs. *Robinson*, Mrs. *Gifford*, Doctor *Trapham's* Family, Mrs. *Fuller*, Mr. *Fyrne*, Mr. *Brawne*, Mr. *Stephens*, Mr. *Rynes* and his Wife, Mr. *Pryor*, Mr. *Lendijeres*, Mr. *Atwell*, Mrs. *Rathorn* and her Family, Mr. *Rynes*. saved by a Boat; but his Wife and the rest of his Children and Family, were all Lost : Several People were Swallow'd up of the Earth, when the Sea breaking in

coffins and corpses. These bobbed on the surface for days, creating such "an intolerable stench that the Dead were like to destroy the Living."[27] Sir Henry Morgan's lead-lined coffin could not float. A tidal wave tore it from the grave and dragged it out to sea. Now it rests somewhere on the bottom, under tons of coral sand.

Broadside depicting the 1692 earthquake that devastated Port Royal.

When the waters receded, the survivors decided to build a new town across the harbor. They called it Kingston.

Today Port Royal lures tourists fascinated by tales of swashbuckling sea rovers. A minor earthquake in 1965 led to the discovery offshore of walls from sunken buildings. Since then, divers have recovered thousands of items buried on that awful day three centuries ago. There are pewter dishes, silver shoe and belt buckles, a gold pocket watch, and hundreds of glass rum bottles. Did some of these belong to Jamaica's most famous citizen? We shall never know.

Yet, in an odd way, Sir Henry Morgan still lives. Elderly fishermen tell a story said to be older than their grandfathers' grandfathers. They are black people, heirs to the island the buccaneers defended and enriched. On dark nights, when the moon hangs in a black velvet sky like a golden doubloon, they say you can hear the distant clanging of a ship's bell. After a while, a shadowy vessel with billowing sails slips over the western horizon.

Skeptics call the vessel a mirage, a trick of the light, a false vision. Those wise in the ways of the sea know better. They claim that the ghostly craft is manned by a ghostly crew armed with cutlasses and pistols. If you take a hard look out there, and use your imagination, you may be lucky. You may see the crew's leader standing on the bridge. A man of medium height and muscular build, he wears his black hair shoulder-length and has a nut brown complexion. Gold rings dangle from his ears, and he carries a pistol inlaid with ivory. . . .

Notes

PROLOGUE: Great Morgan's Fame

1. R. H. Major, trans. and ed., *Select Letters of Christopher Columbus* (New York: Corinth, 1961), 196.

2. Miguel Leon-Portilla, ed., *The Broken Spears: The Aztec Account of the Conquest of Mexico* (Boston: Beacon Press, 1992), 51.

3. See Bartholomé de las Casas, *The Devastation of the Indies: A Brief Account* (Baltimore: The Johns Hopkins University Press, 1992). First published in 1552, las Casas's book detailed horrible atrocities. The European impact on native American populations is the subject of David E. Stannard's *American Holocaust: The Conquest of the New World* (New York: Oxford University Press, 1992), and Kirkpatrick Sale's *The Conquest of Paradise: Christopher Columbus and the Columbian Legacy* (New York: Plume, 1991). On the African slave trade, see Daniel P.

Mannix and Malcolm Cowley, *Black Cargoes: A History of the African Slave Trade: 1518–1865* (London: Longmans, 1962).

4. Spanish coins became so common that other European countries, and later their colonies, accepted them as legal currency. During the American Revolution, some of George Washington's troops were paid with pieces of eight stamped with dates as early as the 1600s.

5. Sir Alan Burns, *History of the British West Indies* (London: George Allen & Unwin, 1954), 139.

CHAPTER ONE: A Passage to America

1. Morgan once gave the year of his birth in a letter sent to a government official in London. There is no record—at least none that has survived—of his ever having written about his parents or discussed them with others.

2. Francis Russell Hart, *Admirals*

of the Caribbean (Boston: Houghton Mifflin, 1935), 105.

3. Dudley Pope, *The Buccaneer King: The Biography of Sir Henry Morgan* (New York: Dodd, Mead & Co., 1977), 64.

4. Carl Bridenbaugh, *Vexed and Troubled Englishmen, 1590–1642* (New York: Oxford University Press, 1968), 62.

5. Ibid., 71–72.

6. Ibid., 150.

7. Ibid., 100.

8. Ibid., 197.

9. Barry Richard Burg. *Sodomy and the Pirate Tradition: English Sea Rovers in the Seventeenth-Century Caribbean* (New York: New York University Press, 1984), 50.

10. Edward Barlow. *Barlow's Journal of His Life at Sea in King's Ships, East and West Indiamen and other Merchantmen from 1659–1703*, ed. Basil Lubbock, 2 vols. (London: Hurst & Blackett, 1934), I, 15, 31.

11. Marcus Rediker, *Between the*

Devil and the Deep Blue Sea: Merchant Seamen, Pirates, and the Anglo-American Maritime World (Cambridge: Cambridge University Press, 1987), 274.

12. Ibid., 10.

13. Burg, *Sodomy and the Pirate Tradition*, 123.

14. *A brief and perfect Journal of The late Proceedings and Success of the English Army in the West Indies, etc., by I.S. and Eye-Witnesse* (London, 1655), 11.

15. Bridenbaugh, *Vexed and Troubled Englishmen*, 11–12.

16. Historians disagree on how Morgan came to the West Indies. Some believe he sailed with the expedition that captured Jamaica in 1655. I follow those who argue that he arrived a year earlier. In this connection, see David Cordingly, *Under the Black Flag: The Romance and Reality of Life among the Pirates* (New York: Random House, 1995), 44; Peter Earle, *The Sack of Panama: Sir Henry Morgan's Adventures on the Spanish Main* (New York: Viking, 1982), 58; Walter Adolphe Roberts, *Sir Henry Morgan* (New York: Covici & Friede, 1933), 48.

17. Barlow, *Journal of His Life at Sea*, I, 60.

18. Peter Kemp, *The British Sailor: A Social History of the Lower Deck* (London: J. M. Dent & Sons, 1970), 12.

19. Rediker, *Between the Devil and the Deep Blue Sea*, 208.

20. Nathaniel Boteler, *A Dialogicall Discourse concerning Marine Affairs betweene The Highie Admirall and a Captaine att Sea* (London, 1634), 27.

21. Kemp, *The British Sailor*, 23.

22. Barlow, *Barlow's Journal of His Life at Sea*, 60–61.

23. Kemp, *The British Sailor*, 4.

24. Bridenbaugh, *Vexed and Troubled Englishmen*, 9.

25. Ibid., 6.

26. Ibid., 7.

27. Ibid., 8.

28. Eric S. Thompson, ed., *Thomas Gage's Travels in the New World* (Westport, CT: Greenwood Press, 1981), 29.

29. Rediker, *Between the Devil and the Deep Blue Sea*, 191.

CHAPTER TWO: The Making of a Buccaneer

1. Carl and Roberta Bridenbaugh, *No Peace Beyond the Line: The English in the Caribbean, 1624–1690* (New York: Oxford University Press, 1972), 122.

2. Pope, *The Buccaneer King*, 157.

3. John Esquemeling, *The Buccaneers of America*, ed. William Swan Stallybrass (London: George Routledge & Sons, 1923), 33.

4. Besides Hispaniola, cimarron communities existed in Mexico, Cuba, Brazil, and along the Spanish Main. In the early days of the United States, blacks fleeing slavery in the Southern states found safety, and intermarried with the Indians, in Spanish-owned Florida. A major reason for the American takeover of Florida was to remove it as a refuge for runaway slaves and to prevent them from crossing the border to rescue others.

5. Rediker, *Between the Devil and the Deep Blue Sea*, 100.

6. Cordingly, *Under the Black Flag*, 9.

7. Esquemeling, *The Buccaneers of America*, 39.

8. In the late 1600s, the "matchlock" musket gave way to the "flintlock," which had a flint set in the hammer for striking a spark to ignite the gunpowder.

9. Esquemeling, *The Buccaneers of America*, 33.

10. Ibid., 57.

11. Ibid.

12. Ibid., 116.

13. Sir Alan Burns, *History of the British West Indies* (London: George Allen & Unwin, 1954), 45.

14. Esquemeling, *The Buccaneers of America*, 59–61.

15. Cordingly, *Under the Black Flag*, 56.

16. Henry J. Webb, *Elizabethan Military Science* (Milwaukee: The University of Wisconsin Press, 1965), 167.

17. Samuel Eliot Morison, *Admiral of the Ocean Sea: A Life of Christopher Columbus* (Boston: Little, Brown, 1942), 451–452.

18. Brigadier General Ernest A.

Cruikshank, *The Life of Sir Henry Morgan* (Toronto: Macmillan, 1935), 8–9.

19. C. H. Haring, *The Buccaneers of the West Indies in the XVII Century* (New York: E. P. Dutton, 1910), 142.

20. Earle, *The Sack of Panama*, 49.

21. Rediker, *Between the Devil and the Deep Blue Sea*, 59.

22. Robert F. Marx, *Pirate Port: The Story of the Sunken City of Port Royal* (Cleveland: The World Publishing Company, 1967), 47.

23. Alexander Winston, *No Man Knows My Name: Sir Henry Morgan, Captain William Kidd, Captain Woodes Rogers in the Age of Privateers and Pirates* (Boston: Houghton Mifflin, 1968), 48.

24. Earle, *The Sack of Panama*, 59.

CHAPTER THREE: Admiral Morgan and His Old Privateers

1. Esquemeling, *The Buccaneers of America*, 131.

2. Morgan kept his promise. As soon as he returned to Jamaica, he hung the murderer from a ship's yardarm for everyone to see.

3. Quoted in David E. Stannard, *American Holocaust: The Conquest of the New World* (New York: Oxford University Press, 1992), 90–91.

4. Thompson, *Thomas Gage's Travels in the New World*, 329–330.

5. Ibid., 330.

6. Esquemeling, *The Buccaneers of America*, 136.

7. Ibid., 143.

8. Earle, *The Sack of Panama*, 43.

9. Esquemeling, *The Buccaneers of America*, 137.

10. Ibid., 139.

11. Ibid., 139–140.

12. Roberts, *Sir Henry Morgan*, 102. Aboard ship, woolding was the rope wound around a mast to give it additional support.

13. Earle, *The Sack of Panama*, 83.

14. Esquemeling, *The Buccaneers of America*, 142.

15. Ibid.

16. Earle, *The Sack of Panama*, 107.

17. Esquemeling, *The Buccaneers of America*, 45.

18. For more information on this fascinating legend, see John Hemming, *The Search for El Dorado* (New York: E. P. Dutton, 1978).

19. Earle, *The Sack of Panama*, 113.

20. Esquemeling, *The Buccaneers of America*, 156.

21. Ibid., 154.

22. Ibid., 160.

23. Earle, *The Sack of Panama*, 124.

24. Esquemeling, *The Buccaneers of America*, 160.

25. Pope, *The Buccaneer King*, 182.

26. Ibid.

27. Esquemeling, *The Buccaneers of America*, 165.

CHAPTER FOUR: The Flames of Panama

1. Samuel Pepys, *Diary*, Robert Latham and William Matthews, eds.(London: G. Bell & Sons, 1970–1973, VII, September 2, 1666).

2. Earle, *The Sack of Panama*, 91.

3. Rosita Forbes, *Henry Morgan, Pirate* (New York: Reynal & Hitchcock, 1946), 55–56.

4. Ibid.

5. Earle, *The Sack of Panama*, 149.

6. Pope, *The Buccaneer King*, 196.

7. Cruikshank, *The Life of Sir Henry Morgan*, 140.

8. Ibid.

9. Earle, *The Sack of Panama*, 180.

10. Thompson, *Thomas Gage's Travels in the New World*, 73. As used here, the words "brave" and "gallant" did not mean courage, but bold and colorful.

11. John Masefield, *On the Spanish Main* (Washington: Naval Institute Press, 1972), 193–194.

12. The English name for Santa Catalina island was Old Providence.

13. Esquemeling, *The Buccaneers of America*, 180.

14. Ibid., 181.

15. Masefield, *On the Spanish Main*, 175.

16. Earle, *The Sack of Panama*,

190; Esquemeling, *The Buccaneers of America*, 187.

17. Esquemeling, *The Buccaneers of America*, 188.

18. Ibid., 192.

19. Ibid., 193.

20. Earle, *The Sack of Panama*, 262.

21. Esquemeling, *The Buccaneers of America*, 195–196.

22. Ibid., 198.

23. Ibid., 199.

24. Ibid.

25. Ibid., 202–203.

26. Ibid., 204.

27. Earle, *The Sack of Panama*, 215.

28. Cruikshank, *The Life of Sir Henry Morgan*, 187.

29. Ibid., 187.

30. Roberts, *Sir Henry Morgan*, 165; Pope, *The Buccaneer King*, 242.

31. Earle, *The Sack of Panama*, 223.

32. Esquemeling, *The Buccaneers of America*, 215.

33. Ibid., 220.

34. Cruikshank, *Sir Henry Morgan*, 198.

CHAPTER 5: Into the Sunset

1. Roberts, *Sir Henry Morgan*, 187.

2. Pope, *The Buccaneer King*, 261.

3. Philip Lindsay, *The Great Buccaneer: Being the Life, Death and Extraordinary Adventures of Sir Henry Morgan, Buccaneer and Lieutenant Governor of Jamaica* (New York: Wilfred Funk, Inc., 1951), 137.

4. The king also freed Sir Thomas Modyford and made him chief justice of Jamaica, where he died in 1679. No portrait or description of Sir Henry Morgan's greatest ally survives.

5. Charles Leslie, *History of Jamaica* (London: J. H. Hodges, 1740), 28–29.

6. Bridenbaugh, *No Peace Beyond the Line*, 350.

7. Ibid., 351.

8. Everild Young and Kjeld Helwig-Larsen, eds., *The Pirate's Priest: The Life of Pére Labat in the West Indies, 1693–1705* (London: Jarrolds, 1965), 127.

9. Masefield, *On the Spanish Main*, 216.

10. Lionel Wafer, *A New Voyage and Desription of the Isthmus of Panama* (Oxford: Oxford University Press, 1934), 73.

11. Lindsay, *The Great Buccaneer*, 227.

12. Cruikshank, *Sir Henry Morgan*, 326.

13. Ibid., 341.

14. Winston. *No Man Knows My Name*, 95.

15. Pope, *The Buccaneer King*, 330.

16. Ibid., 329.

17. Ibid.

18. Morgan's disgrace gave Lynch only momentary pleasure. He died the following year, 1684, heartbroken over the death by drowning of his beloved wife and their two sons.

19. Bridenbaugh, *No Peace Beyond the Line*, 142–143.

20. Sir Hans Sloane, *Voyage to Jamaica*, 2 vols. (London: Printed by B.M. for the Author, 1707), I, xcviii.

21. Cruikshank, *Sir Henry Morgan*, 416.

22. King Charles II died in 1685 and his successor, his brother James, was overthrown by Parliament during the "Glorious Revolution" which broke out toward the end of 1688.

23. Sloane, *Voyage to Jamaica*, I, xcviii.

24. Ibid., I, xcix.

25. Dr. Heath wrote the best account we have of the disaster. Printed in London during the winter of 1692, he called it *A Full Account of the late dreadful Earthquake at Port Royall in Jamaica, written in two letters from the minister of that place, from aboard the Grenada in Port Royall Harbour.* In describing the earthquake, I have relied upon this unpaged pamphlet.

26. Ibid.

27. Bridenbaugh, *No Peace Beyond the Line*, 190.

More Books About
Sir Henry Morgan and His Times

Andrews, Kenneth R. *The Spanish Caribbean*. New Haven, CT: Yale University Press, 1978.

Arciniegas, Germán. *Caribbean: Sea of the New World*. New York: Knopf, 1946.

Barlow, Edward. *Barlow's Journal of His Life at Sea in King's Ships, East and West Indiamen and other Merchantmen from 1659–1703*, edited by Basil Lubbock. 2 vols., London: Hurst & Blackett, 1934.

Besson, Maurice. *The Scourge of the Indies*. New York: Random House, 1929.

Braley, Berton. *Morgan Sails the Caribbean*. New York: Macmillan, 1934.

Bridenbaugh, Carl. *Vexed and Troubled Englishmen, 1590–1642*. New York: Oxford University Press, 1968.

Bridenbaugh, Carl and Roberta. *No Peace Beyond the Line: The English in the Caribbean, 1624–1690*. New York: Oxford University Press, 1972.

Burg, Barry Richard. *Sodomy and the Pirate Tradition: English Sea Rovers in the Seventeenth-Century Caribbean*. New York: New York University Press, 1984.

Burns, Sir Alan. *History of the British West Indies*. London: George Allen & Unwin, 1954.

Cooper-Pritchard, A. H. *The Buccaneers*. London: Cecil Palmer, 1927.

Cordingly, David. *Under the Black Flag: The Romance and Reality of Life among the Pirates*. New York: Random House, 1995.

Cruikshank, Brigadier General Ernest A. *The Life of Sir Henry Morgan*. Toronto: Macmillan, 1935.

Earle, Peter. *The Sack of Panama: Sir Henry Morgan's Adventures on the Spanish Main*. New York: Viking, 1982.

Esquemeling, John. *The Buccaneers of America*, ed. William Swan Stallybrass. London: George Routledge & Sons, 1923.

Forbes, Rosita. *Henry Morgan, Pirate*. New York: Reynal & Hitchcock, 1946.

Hamshire, C. E. "Henry Morgan and the Buccaneers," *History Today*, XVI (1966), 406–14.

Hanke, Lewis. *The Spanish Struggle for Justice in the Conquest of America*. Boston: Little, Brown and Co., 1965.

Haring, C. H. *The Buccaneers of the West Indies in the XVII Century*. New York: E. P. Dutton, 1910.

Hart, Francis Russell. *Admirals of the Caribbean*. Boston: Houghton Mifflin, 1935.

Jobé, Joseph, ed. *The Great Age of Sail*. Greenwich, CT: Edita Lausanne, 1967.

Kemp, Peter. *The British Sailor: A Social History of the Lower Deck*. London: J. M. Dent & Sons, 1970.

Kemp, P. K., and Christopher Lloyd. *The Brethren of the Coast*. London: Heinemann, 1960.

Lindsay, Philip. *The Great Buccaneer: Being the Life, Death and Extraordinary Adventures of Sir Henry Morgan, Buccaneer and Lieutenant Governor of Jamaica*. New York: Wilfred Funk, Inc., 1951.

Mannix, Daniel P., and Malcolm Cowley. *Black Cargoes: A History of the Atlantic Slave Trade, 1518–1865*. London: Longmans, 1962.

Marley, David F. *Pirates and Privateers of the Americas*. Santa Barbara, CA, 1994.

Marx, Robert F. *Pirate Port: The Story of the Sunken City of Port Royal*. Cleveland: World Publishing Company, 1967.

———. *The Treasure Fleets of the Spanish Main*. Cleveland: World Publishing Co., 1968.

Masefield, John. *On the Spanish Main*. Washington: Naval Institute Press, 1972 [1906].

Means, P. A. *The Spanish Main*. New York: Scribner's, 1935.

Mirchell, David. *Pirates*. New York: The Dial Press, 1976.

Newton, Arthur Percival. *The European Nations in the West Indies, 1493–1688*. London: A & C Black, 1933.

Parry, John Horace. *The Age of Reconnaissance: Discovery, Exploration, and Settlement, 1450–1650*. Cleveland: World Publishing Company, 1963.

———. *The Spanish Seaborne Empire*. New York: Knopf, 1970.

——— and P. M. Sherlock. *A Short History of the West Indies*. London: Macmillan, 1966.

Pawson, Michael, and David Buisseret. *Port Royal, Jamaica*. Oxford: The Clarendon Press, 1975.

Peterson, Mendel. *The Funnel of Gold*. Boston: Little, Brown and Co., 1975.

Pike, Ruth. *Enterprise and Adventure*. Ithaca: Cornell University Press, 1966.

Pond, Seymour G. *True Adventures of Pirates*. Boston: Little, Brown and Co., 1954.

Pope, Dudley. *The Buccaneer King: The Biography of Sir Henry Morgan*. New York: Dodd, Mead & Co., 1977.

Pringle, Patrick. *The Jolly Roger: The Story of the Great Age of Piracy*. New York: W. W. Norton, 1953.

Pyle, Howard. *Book of Pirates*. New York: Harper & Bros., 1921.

Rediker, Marcus. *Between the Devil and the Deep Blue Sea: Merchant Seamen, Pirates, and the Anglo-American Maritime World*. Cambridge: Cambridge University Press, 1987.

Roberts, Walter Adolphe. *The French in the West Indies*. New York: Cooper Square Publishers, 1971.

———. *Sir Henry Morgan*. New York: Covici & Friede, 1933.

Rodger, N.A.M. *The Wooden World: An Anatomy of the Georgian Navy*. Annapolis, MD: Naval Institute Press, 1986.

Senior, Clive. *A Nation of Pirates: English Piracy in Its Heyday*. London: David and Charles, 1976.

Stannard, David E. *American Holocaust: The Conquest of the New World*. New York: Oxford University Press, 1992.

Sternbeck, Alfred. *Filibusters and Buccaneers*. New York: Robert M. McBride & Co., no date.

Thompson, Eric S. *Thomas Gage's Travels in the New World*. Westport, CT: Greenwood Press, 1981.

Thornton, Arthur P. "The Modyfords and Morgan," *Jamaican Historical Review*, 2 (1952), 36–60.

Wafer, Lionel. *A New Voyage and Description of the Isthmus of Panama*. Oxford: Oxford University Press, 1934.

Wertenbaker, Thomas L. *The First Americans, 1607–1690*. Chicago: Quadrangle Books, 1971 [1927].

Whipple, A.B.C. *Pirate: Rascals of the Spanish Main*. Garden City, NY: Doubleday & Co., 1957.

Winston, Alexander. *No Man Knows My Name: Sir Henry Morgan, Captain William Kidd, Captain Woodes Rogers in the Age of Privateers and Pirates*. Boston: Houghton Mifflin, 1969.

Wood, Peter. *The Spanish Main*. Chicago: Time-Life Books, 1979.

Woodbury, George. *The Great Days of Piracy in the West Indies*. New York: W. W. Norton, 1951.

Young, Everild, and Kjeld Helwig-Larsen. *The Pirate's Priest: The Life of Père Labat in the West Indies, 1693–1705*. London: Jarrolds, 1965.

Index

About the Author

ALBERT MARRIN has written over two dozen highly acclaimed non-fiction books for young people. He is chairman of the history department at Yeshiva University in New York City. Prior to teaching on the college level, he worked for nine years as a social studies teacher in a public junior high school in New York City. Dr. Marrin received the Washington Children's Books Guild and *Washington Post* Non-Fiction Award for an "outstanding lifetime contribution [that] has enriched the field of children's literature." Two of his books, 1812: *The War Nobody Won* and *Unconditional Surrender: Ulysses S. Grant and the Civil War*, were named *Boston Globe-Horn Book* Honor Books. *Unconditional Surrender* also won the Dorothy Canfield Fisher Children's Books Award. His previous book for Dutton Children's Books, *Commander in Chief Abraham Lincoln and the Civil War*, was a *Booklist* Children's Editors' Choice. A native New Yorker, Albert Marrin lives with his wife, Yvette, in New York City.